Living More
Than OK

Living More Than OK

Spiraling Up To Abundant Living

Frank Coulson M. Ed., M. Div., LPC

authorHOUSE®

AuthorHouse™ LLC
1663 Liberty Drive
Bloomington, IN 47403
www.authorhouse.com
Phone: 1-800-839-8640

Published by AuthorHouse   10/14/2013

ISBN: 978-1-4918-2831-1 (sc)
ISBN: 978-1-4918-2832-8 (hc)
ISBN: 978-1-4918-2833-5 (e)

Library of Congress Control Number: 2013918236

Any people depicted in stock imagery provided by Thinkstock are models, and such images are being used for illustrative purposes only.
Certain stock imagery © Thinkstock.

This book is printed on acid-free paper.

Contents

Foreword...vii

1. The Problem of Just Existing—Boredom.......................... 1
2. Why Consider Living More Than OK? 12
3. The Importance of Becoming A Bookhead 21
4. Living More Than OK Using Critical Thinking 30
5. Tapping Into Your Creativity 44
6. Making The Most Of Your Time/Savoring Life 60
7. Be Open To Happenstance.......................................80
8. Dream Big and Reach Your Goals 94
9. Walking the Pride and Arrogance Tightrope (Self Esteem) 107
10. Don't Stay On The Mat—Bounce Back With Resilience.......118
11. Spiritual Beings In A Material World 140
12. Follow Your Purpose With Passion...............................159
13. Aim For Natural Highs 177
14. Thankfulness As A Lifestyle 197
15. Take a Risk For More Possibilities..............................209

Final Thoughts...227

Foreword

This book is a culmination of the past few years of work within a blog I have been writing—www.livingmorethanok.blogspot. com. The idea of the blog came to me after taking an online course on the subject of Positive Psychology which had been an interest of mine. I am grateful for the opportunity I had to take the course which followed the lectures of Dr. Tal Ben-Shahar's famous course at Harvard on Positive Psychology. At the end of the course lectures Dr. Ben-Shahar encouraged those taking the course to promote positive psychology so I came up with the idea for the blog. My blog just isn't about positive psychology completely, I discuss career issues and spirituality issues as well as those are topics that interest me as well.

As for the title, Living More Than OK: Spiraling Up To Abundant Living there are two key thoughts behind it. The first part, Living More Than OK is of course from my blog title. The idea comes from my observing people and my own experience. During my own most difficult times in life inside I knew I was merely existing. Yet when people would ask how I was doing on those most difficult days I would smile and say, "I'm OK". I see too much of that in the world. Instead of living their own dreams people waste time watching what is termed "Reality TV", (which is not really reality). They live their dreams out vicariously through those programs instead of enjoying an abundant life by being active in personal growth and personal creativity. Too many just exist instead of enjoying life.

As for the subtitle of Spiraling Up To Abundant Living, that relates to my listening to the lectures of Dr. Tal Ben-Shahar. In one lecture he was speaking of the common phrase, a downward spiral". I was accustomed with that phrase in work with addicts as their drug use causes a downward spiral to deeper negativity. He put a positive spin on the phrase by saying that positive psychology desires to help all people spiral upwards to greater heights in their life journey. I was initially surprised at the concept, then realized he was right. No matter where we are at on the continuum of our mental and spiritual growth we can keep spiraling up to higher levels of growth. If we do not keep growing we settle into OKness which leads to stagnation and merely getting by. So the call of this book is to encourage continual spiraling up to deeper abundant living.

A little about the book, you will quickly see this in not an in-depth book on positive psychology. My desire in writing this book is to amalgamate the posts from my blog into a series of lite essays to hopefully wet your mental and emotional appetite to dig deeper into the resources I list on the various topics. Since I am a Bookhead, I will share many books that I have learned from and feel are profitable for personal growth. What is a Bookhead? I will share that later. At the end of each chapter I include reflection questions. I would suggest purchasing a journal at your local office supply store or book store and at the end of each chapter work through some of the questions or better yet, all the questions to gain more personal insight on the topics. The format of this first book of mine is to be simple like my blog is. So you will simply see breaks between the paragraphs with no indents to give it the feel of how I do my blog.

One difference in this book relates to my love of music. In many of the chapters I will be mentioning various songs that I feel relate to the topic. This relates to my belief that music and songs can have a powerful influence in our lives. Knowing that we are in a technological age and many people have an electronic device with them at all times, I am trying something different. I will simply state the title of the song and mention my thoughts about the song. Instead of listing lyrics, I encourage you to go to YouTube or Vimeo and search for the videos of the songs. I feel experientially, you as a reader, may gain more personal insight into the songs by actually listening to them on the web.

I want to state a worldview disclaimer in this Forward. I do come at my writing from a Christian worldview. That is the rose colored glasses I wear in my thinking. So in relation to your beliefs you may not agree fully with all I say. That is fine, as in my years of reading as a Bookhead, there are many times I have disagreed with an author. Yet I try to glean truths out of each book to help in my life journey. I believe if you are agnostic, Buddhist, Jewish, Muslim, or any other belief system there are principles you can learn and grow from in my book. That is the important issue—keep growing and spiraling up in your life.

You will also see this book is not stating that there are 5 or 6 easy steps to a miraculous life. I have read books like that and do enjoy many of the ideas I have learned from them. Personally I believe we are uniquely created as individuals, so we all grow to higher levels of Living More Than OK in different ways. Some of the topics here in my book may touch your heart and mind in a deeper way than the next reader. That points to our uniqueness. Those topics that internally stand out to you I would encourage you do further study on them.

Before jumping into the essays I want to mention some thanks! I dedicate this book to my third grade teacher and her husband, Verna and Parke Clifford. Verna was an amazing teacher that I am thankful I had in third grade at Woodford Elementary in Barberton, Ohio. She was and still is an encourager. She encouraged each student into their own strengths. She also emphasized the importance of reading and writing. I am glad my mother kept in touch with her over the years so I could then keep in touch throughout the years as well. Her husband, Parke, is a fellow Bookhead, who is now doing his reading in Heaven. We as a family had the pleasure to visit him a couple years back during his final days is hospice. He like his wife, was amazing. He was an example of dying well. Nurses several times had to come in and quiet the party atmosphere that Parke created in the room as he was waiting to pass on to the other side. They both as a couple in my mind are examples of Living More Than OK, as they always were upbeat and growing in their personal lives and touching others in positive ways.

I also want to thank dear friends who have encouraged me in my writing over the past few years. Their prayers and kind feedback have been appreciated. I am also thankful for the authors of the books I mention here in this book and other books on my bookshelves that have helped stimulate my thinking and challenge my thinking over the years. I also thank you as a reader for taking time to be on the journey of Living More Than OK. My hope is that you glean insights to keep you spiraling up in your personal growth. Last but not least, I want to thank my wife, Myungsook, and daughter, Alejandra, for their support and encouragement in putting up with my passion for reading and writing.

I would be amiss if I did not thank the staff at Authorhouse, as they all have been wonderful to work with on my first book project. I need to thank as well a dear artist friend, Linda Shum, who created the logo you see at the top of the front cover.

The Problem of Just Existing—Boredom

Why would a person begin their book looking at the subject of boredom? My thoughts on living a more than ok life relates to my observation over the years that too many of us do not live up to all the potential we have in us. Throughout my life I have been more of an introverted observer of life around me and the people around me. Through all the various stages of life I have seen boredom as a part of what I call living just an ok existence. It is merely getting by or just existing.

Most everyone remembers growing up and going to school and either observed or even experienced boredom in school. Of course the levels of boredom varied from student to student. I will admit I experienced this boredom as well even though I believe I experienced it less than some as I will mention in a future chapter. There were some teachers who would make education come alive and some with whom we just endured the time boringly watching for the clock to reach 3:15pm for the end of the school day. One reason as students Summer was so exciting is it meant a break from school. Yet even today I will speak with parents who state their children by the end of Summer are bored at home and look forward to school again. I remember that same feeling.

One of my early jobs in between my college years was working shipping and receiving at a company in Ohio. My work setting was fast-paced so the day would often go quickly. During slow periods though, the hours would drag on as if they would never end. In this setting I would observe my fellow workers who were bored as well.

For many the main focus of their lives came across as waiting for 5 pm on Friday to get their paychecks and rush out to the bars. Just to do the whole routine the following week. Many people are the same just living for the weekend. They keep the cycle going of just existing week by week.

Later after college, I would see this attitude in companies I would work at in the Chicago area as well. I observed too many living lives of quiet desperation and boredom. This reminded me of the quote by Henry David Thoreau "Most men lead lives of quiet desperation and go to the grave with the song still in them." There seemed to be no passion or meaning to life. People's existence of simply going through the workday cycle and getting a little pleasure on the weekend. I found myself thinking—is this all there is to life? Is this the way we were meant to live? Of course growing up as a Christian I personally believed the statement of Christ, "I am come that you may have life, and keep on having it in abundance" John 10:10. So that meant to me that we were meant to live better than working day in and day out with a little respite on the weekend. This was the beginning of my thinking that we are meant to live more than OK.

My primary reading and research on boredom began about 10 years ago. I began reading up on the issue of boredom and life. This resulted from an encounter I had with a student in my office for Career Counseling, who happened to be struggling with his classes. In the discussion of what was the main problem other than uncertainty on a career focus, he mentioned that he was easily bored with his classes, especially the liberal arts basic courses. Boredom would overtake him and he would start skipping class. Over the next couple years, I informally kept track of students who brought up boredom as a negative effect on their education and life. Within one semester alone at least 14 students brought up the issue of boredom as a major factor in their difficulty with college. They all happened to be on probation for their grades. As I read literature on boredom, it affirmed what I was seeing in some of the students, that boredom can negatively affect students' progress.

Also in a College Success course I taught for Freshman students, I would do a variety of reflection statements. Their responses on lack of purpose and passion probably remains the most important force in my thinking behind this book concerning living life more than ok. I have spoken with many students over the past 10 years who struggle with their grades because they are bored with college. I would be a rich man if I had a dollar for every time I have heard the word bored from students on the campuses I have worked on in the past years. In discussing boredom further with some of the students it is often because they lack a sense of meaning in life or do not have a set direction. They are just like the workers at the company who were just living week end to week end. I also observed a connection with the media driven age we live in, so the students are bombarded with stimulation on all the videos and TV shows they watch. So they easily become bored when the rest of life is not that stimulating.

On one reflection as to why students are not proactive in seeking help one student's comment stood out to me. She stated, "Some, like me, feel we should be able to handle what life throws at us. Then when overwhelmed we don't seek help because we will slough through it." Her thoughts reminded me again of Thoreau's' view of people living "lives of quiet desperation." Just getting by, just existing, which corresponds to my thought of just living ok. Those who state that famous quote of Thoreau often neglect the end of that quote which is the most important part—"go to the grave with the song still in them." That song is the abundant living. Learning to live out the song that has been put in the hearts of all of us makes life more than ok. That is one hope I have in writing this book that readers can move beyond sloughing through life and tap into their song of abundant living.

In all of my reading books and articles about boredom a quote that struck me about boredom is from Lars Svendsen, a Philosophy professor in Norway. In his book *A Philosophy of Boredom* he states—"Boredom is inhuman as it robs human life of meaning, or possibly it is an expression of the fact that such a meaning is absent." (page 33). I like how Dr. Svendsen mentions that a life of boredom robs our lives of meaning. When reading his description of the effects of boredom on our life existence I pictured in my mind a dry desert with cracks in the ground, dry craggy rocks and withered brown brush. This is how I view people's lives who are just existing in life—all dried up with no vitality. The life of boredom is as dry and lifeless as a desert. No excitement or passion along with the thought of robbing our lives of meaning.

Research studies and books about boredom show that boredom is related to a host of negative problems that face us in destroying our human potential. Boredom relates closely to depression and anxiety disorders. Boredom does not equal these mental and emotional maladies but is often a precursor. Prolonged boredom can turn into these disorders. Loneliness, and a sense of hopelessness in life are factors that relate to boredom. Boredom also affects the sense of meaning and purpose we have in our life journey. Much of Lars Svendsen's book relates to the connection between the lack of purpose and meaning and the increased levels of boredom in a person's life.

Boredom has been shown to lead to risky behaviors. Criminals behavior among juveniles occur often due to boredom. They are seeking ways to combat boredom so wind up doing crimes to break out of the boredom. This then can spiral then down a path to more crime. Also much of the research on alcohol and drug abuse is seen as a way people are trying to counter boredom. They are looking for an easy quick way to feel excitement. The problem is the easy quick fix leads to the ensuing addictions which then lead to deeper problems. So boredom relates to increased negativity in life.

In my work with college students I always emphasize there is so much potential in life for their personal fulfillment and doing great things. Are we robbing ourselves from all that life can offer by living boring lives of just ok? How can we reach for more potential in our lives and live more that OK? Just the word ok is intriguing to me. In naming my blog, which is the basis of this book; I thought how I often respond "OK" when I am asked how I am doing. But isn't living just OK beneath our potential? Isn't OK living kind of boring? Living in boredom is living in a cloudy maze similar to a depressive fog. Just OK living is going through the motions with no purpose or meaning. I remember during my most difficult times in my life as I would be asked How are you doing? I would smile and say I am doing OK. The outward experience did not match the inner reality.

In the book *Amusing Ourself to Death*, the author brings up that our oversaturated media culture has helped create higher levels of boredom. People in our media driven age need to be stimulated almost continually or they become bored. Attention spans have been reduced to the point that people can not take time to enjoy the roses on the journey of life. They can't take the time to listen. They can't take the time to enjoy the scenery around them. It is rush, rush but where are they going. Just a boring rush from one place to the next. Their lives are not improving they are just existing in ok mode. This is what I have observed in the experience of people I have worked with and students I have helped. They can be going through difficulties and say everything is alright but it is not alright. Just existing or going through hurts is not the way life is meant to be.

We are meant for more. We were created for a better life. The statement of Jesus comes to mind, "The thief does not come except to steal, and to kill, and to destroy. I have come that they may have life and that they may have it more abundantly." John 10:10. This is more the way I think we should be living life. Abundant living is living life to the fullest. Boredom as the earlier quote states is a robber that steals from our living and destroys and in some cases sadly, even kills. Abundant living helps us to live to our fullest God given potential. This book seeks to explore how we can move beyond boredom to living a joyful and abundant life? The journey we were meant to live.

In being open and accepting of our humanness we need to be aware from the previous discussion, that in our life journey letting boredom control us into living in ok mode has a tendency to make messes in our lives. At times we are our own worst enemy towards living an abundant life which I term Living More Than OK. We fall into wrong behaviors or harmful thought patterns that affect our behaviors. Sometimes it is a negative reaction to chance events in our lives.

As I look at my life journey overall I have had low levels of boredom but there was a time period where the levels were dangerously high. There was a point in time where I was in a stressful work environment at the same time I was experience difficulties in a personal relationship. At that same time period my mother passed away from a stroke. Then the very next year I had an older brother, who was mentally disabled due to an early childhood accident and later substance abuse; diagnosed with end stage lung cancer. He had been a chain smoker since his teen years so it wasn't a surprise. Yet with mom gone it fell on my shoulders to be making end of life decisions for him. I was in Chicago and he was in a nursing home in Akron, Ohio so with work stressful I did not need the pressure of traveling back and forth but he was my brother. Thankfully I had a cousin who was a nurse at the facility where my brother's final days were that was an emotional help to him and myself. After my brother died, work became more of a stressor which caused me to crash emotionally as I had not really dealt with the relationship problem, mom's death, and my older brother's death. Everything had been masked by keeping busy at work. For me this time was of just existing and I had moved more into depression. At work people during this whole time period of personal difficulties would ask how I was doing? I would always respond with a false smile, "I'm doing OK."

This all led up to a personal crash that was more of a deep depression, where I was too dysfunctional to work and simply stayed reclusive in my apartment. As previously stated boredom is closely linked to depression. The clouded mind, the heavy no hope spirit that weighs one down as if a heavy chain is wrapped around the body immobilizing the self. The next six months was staying in my apartment and about the only time in my life I ever watched a talk show on television. To me that was the epitome of boredom. Reduced to watching daytime talk shows. I think I even watched Oprah once. Much of the literature on boredom focuses in on the lack of meaning and purpose. I experienced that during this time period. Often wondering if life was worth living and even one time considering ending it all as I felt, what was the use of going on in life that was simply pain and loneliness.

One evening when I was at my worst I kept mulling over what is the purpose of living in such a life. I had stopped socializing at the church I had attended and my life was just a monotonous 24 hours a day in my Chicago apartment. It was also middle of Winter which can be depressing enough in Chicago with day after day of grey cloudy skies. In the middle of my evening on this most despondent day, I heard the apartment buzzer sound. For the past few days I had been ignoring phone calls and apartment buzzers. I decided to check it out. It was a Korean Pastor and his wife from one of the churches I had been attending. They were asking me out to dinner. I reluctantly agreed. The conversation that night worked as a tipping point wake up call to start relooking at meaning that God had for me to attend to in my life.

The wake up call started me in realizing ending it all was not the answer. I started to rebound as I reconnected with my social network in the churches I had been attending. Also I knew the importance of Counseling so I sought out a Counselor to work on the issues I had been burying. During the 6 months of reclusiveness it dawned on me I had not been reading which had always been a big part of my life so I used some bibliotherapy in reading books relevant to the issues I had been enduring in my life journey. During that difficult period as well, I took the time to reflect on how I wanted the rest of my life to go. Times of meditation on the Psalms and solitude of prayerful reflection on my life journey helped me make better Choices. A quote that meant much to me at this time was "Listen to the quietest of whispers of your mind . . . They are telling you the choices that will help you the most." (Dr. Shad Helmstetter). It is during times of quiet solitude where we can think through our lives and our future possibilities with deeper clarity.

As I mentioned in the forward I believe in the power of music. There is power for good and bad. I enjoy instrumental music and lyrical songs that have a positive or spiritual message and believe we can learn from songs. In relation to this chapter on boredom and just existing, I want to share first of all a song by the metal band RED, called *Break Me Down* which speaks to me about the battle of boredom. I felt the lyrics were descriptive of the sense of nothingness, being trapped in the shadows that we experience when we are controlled by boredom. The phrase, "I find a stranger trapped within" fits well with boredom as when boredom is with us too long we do feel strange, as that is not the way we were created to be.

I am trying something in this book that in most chapters I will mention songs that I find insightful about life. I will just present some ideas about the songs. Hopefully that will entice you the reader, to go to the internet as all the songs I mention have videos on either Youtube.com or Vimeo.com. View the videos of the songs I mention and reflect your own thoughts of what the songs are saying. I feel hearing actual songs will have more meaning to you. You can even simply place the song titles in your favorite search engine as well such as Google or Bing and find videos of the songs as well. So I hope you go the extra mile and try this idea out.

Here are some of my thoughts from the lyrics as I think over our battle with boredom in life, We were made by our Creator to be people who have a need to find ourselves. We desire meaning as we have innate curiosity to grow and learn and explore new things. Observe young children, their eyes are always darting about looking at new objects in their environment with a deep curiosity. Boredom keeps us trapped in the shadows of our comfort zone and hinders us from exploring new ideas, new places, new environments, new books. Just existing makes the individual feel like nothingness is controlling them. The need is felt to break free of the sense of nothingness.

The song speaks of wanting to shine. We were created to "shine". God has given each of us talents and natural gifts to help us enjoy life more and to brighten the lives of others around us. But instead of shining with the talents we have our lives our dulled by the feelings of nothingness in boredom. It tells us there is nothing special about us, that we can't do anything. There is that word can't again. By breaking out of the nothingness of boredom we are free to shine in our talents so as to enjoy our life journey better and our shine can help brighten others lives.

Another aspiration placed in us by our Creator is to "rise". We all want to be noticed and be recognized. Arrogance takes this aspiration to the extreme. At that point we are usually outwardly or inwardly disdained by others. There is nothing wrong with rising above the okness of life. There is nothing wrong in improving our talents and striving for excellence. On a trip one weekend I spoke with a cheerful hotel worker about my blog Living More Than OK. She liked the title as she said she felt really great about her level of spirituality but the other areas of her life she admitted were just ok not really flourishing. I believe we can keep rising in a balanced way in all areas of our lives.

The song kept repeating the phrase, "Break me down". I am not sure what the artists mean by that. I see it in the sense of taking an honest look at where we are at. As I have mentioned before boredom is a sign post trying to tell us either to take time to chill out and enjoy the present moment, or time to make a change in our lives. Break out and try something new. The essays in the following chapters will provide ideas to humbly view ourselves and break free to abundant living.

One other song that comes to mind with this chapter on boredom comes from a singer songwriter that my wife, daughter and I enjoy— Matthew West. His song *The Motions*, speaks to me of moving beyond the boredom, the sameness, the going through the motions that keep us from living a flourishing, abundant life. You will find several very good videos done in relation to this song on the internet.

The dull routines of our individual rat race often leaves us feeling like we are just going through the motions each day. The feeling is kind of like the Movie, *Ground Hog Day*, where the day keeps happening over and over again. Matthew West captures the description of the desperate boring life many people find themselves trapped in, "Cause just ok is not enough, help me fight through the nothingness of life." This is the life over the years I have seen students and others ensnared in and I have had my times of experiencing it as well. It is the "Just OK" life that keeps us living far below the potential that each of us have in us. It is the life that tricks us into seeing our work as just a job to grunt through, rather than a calling. It is a life that causes us to waste so much time staring at mind numbing TV shows or even nonsensical, inane Youtube videos for hours at a time.

The song, The Motions, reminds me of the power of choice. We have a choice to make how we live our lives. Are we going to stay in the numbing comfort of the recliner and live just ok? Or are we willing to take a risk to step out to make a difference in life? Matthew West as a Christian is pointing to letting the passionate love of God to consume and control our lives. As a follower of this worldview I whole heartedly concur. Yet the principle of breaking out of the "unfeeling ok", existence to finding a passionate purpose to take control of our living, can be expanded in many ways in each of our journeys. Christians and non–Christians can live lives of passion for maximum potential living and having no regrets in life. The key is making the right choices to move from just ok to more than ok.

Reflections:

Take some time in a quiet setting to reflect over the areas of your life where you feel like you are going through the motions. Jot those areas down on a paper, journal, or computer document. Then brainstorm some solutions and ideas to break out of the rut. Also in the brainstorming consider if there is a passion for something that you would like to take the risk to branch out into in your present life journey?

What is your talent you have where you wish to rise and shine?

How can you get back to being the you—you want to be?

What will help you make your life more alive?

Resources for further learning:

Krasko, Genrich, This Unbearable Boredom of Being, I Universe Inc. 2004

RED, "Break Me Down", *End of Silence* CD, 2006

Sommers, Jennifer & Vodanovich, Stephen J.; Boredome proness: Its Relationship to Psychological and Physical Health Symptoms; Journal of Clinical Psychology; Vol 56:1; pgs 149–155. 2000.

Svendsen, Lars, A Philosophy of Boredom, Reaktion Books, 2005

West, Mathew "The Motions", *Something to Say* CD, 2009

Winter, Richard, Still Bored In A Culture of Entertainment, Intervarsity Press, 2002

Why Consider Living More Than OK?

This book and my desire to see people live more than OK in their life journey, has been years in the making. The primary impetus was the result of taking an online Positive Psychology course featuring the lectures of Dr. Tal Ben-Shahar that I mentioned in the Forward section. The first chapter I focused on one of the main problems I see in modern life that of too many people living in a boring existence of just getting by. My thoughts on how to help people move beyond this state had its initial starting point in my teen years being an avid reader I would read psychology and personal self-help books such as I'm OK You're OK and The Road Less Travelled, Partly to over come my own low self-image with the desire to improve my life. Psychology interested me as it spoke to helping people overcoming mental illnesses of depression, anxieties, and fears.

Reading a book by Dr. Martin Seligman, *Authentic Happiness*, challenged to see how what he called Positive Psychology, could enhance everyone's life not just those struggling with mental illnesses. Years after reading his book I had the opportunity to take an online class by Dr. Tal Ben-Shahar on Positive Psychology. In his lectures he spoke of how Dr. William James and Dr. Abraham Maslow in the past had focused not on illness but how to make lives better for all by studying positive human characteristics. He repeated a phrase that stuck in my mind about helping people spiral upwards. That caught me off guard, as I had often heard about people spiraling downwards. People who do not get help for their problems and spin out of control are often described as going into a downward spiral. I felt Dr. Ben-Shahar was right if someone can spiral down negatively, why can't they spiral upwards in improving their lives in a positive direction. His course in my mind's eye was eye-opening as how we can use the principles of positive psychology to help people, all people spiral upwards to improved lives.

That is what I desire from this book. To look at a variety of positive psychology principles and other topics that interest me and in short essays show how they can be used to better all of our lives. Again as I mentioned in the first chapter, I feel we were not put on this earth just to exist and get by in what I call OK mode. We are here on this journey to Live More Than OK. To keep spiraling upwards to abundant living. The journey looks different for each person. That is why I am not emphasizing 5 or 7 magic ways to reach abundant living. I have read numerous books that speak of the 5 or 6 magic ways to live an amazing life. "If you follow my five principles health and wealth will drop out of the sky into your life" is what the authors often say. I am sure they work for some but I believe we are all created uniquely different and are given different purposes on our journeys. Therefore I don't believe we can all fit into the same 3 or 5 key secret cookie cutter molds for success. I am not knocking those type of books as there is much to learn from the authors ideas and passions.

Instead the chapters ahead will look at many standard ideas found in Positive Psychology and probably some that would not be considered standard parts of Positive Psychology. The parts that do not relate to positive psychology are included because I have found them important in my life journey and also since this is my book I feel I can put them in. I don't expect every reader to agree with everything I present as we are all on different journeys. But I believe though I present enough varied principles that anyone can find a few new concepts to help them spiral upwards in a positive direction in their life.

Another book by Dr. Seligman, *Flourish*, helped me see the importance of Positive Psychology for helping those on their life journeys to have the best journey possible. His book, *Flourish* is a deeper expansion of Positive Psychology beyond his initial work,

Authentic Happiness. He shows examples of how the principles behind Positive Psychology have been used with beneficial results in a variety of populations. He shows in research and examples how Positive Psychology principles promote flourishing lives.

The deeper expansion Dr. Seligman speaks of in the book is moving beyond happiness to overall improved well being in our human life journey. The core features of Positive Psychology he mentions in the first chapter are having positive emotions, being intentionally engaged in our life focus, and having a sense of meaning and purpose. The first core principle focuses in on our happiness level and life satisfaction. The second core principle is centered on the joy of learning and creatively looking at life. Then the third focuses in on what is the big picture of what we want to do with our lives. What will make our life journey meaningful? We will be looking into these principles throughout the chapters of this book.

In the preface of the book he makes this statement that stood out to me ". . . happiness, flow, meaning, love, gratitude, accomplishment, growth, better relationships—constitute human flourishing. Learning that you can have more of these things is life changing." Life can be a continual growing journey of flourishing if we make the right choices to spiral up instead of spiral down in life. This is the way to have the best life possible and I believe it is the way we were meant to be Living More Than OK.

I do want to say again upfront in case you missed reading the Forward, that I come at life with a Christian worldview. We all look at life from our own worldview. I read books by authors from various worldviews, from Christian, Eastern Philosophy, to Secular Humanistic to seek to gain what truths I can glean for my benefit. I hope if you are reading this from an agnostic or other religious point of view you will find numerous truths to help in your life journey. That being said, the title of Dr. Seligman's book made me personally think of analogies in the Bible that relate to flourishing as to how God wants us to be living. I looked in the scriptures for the word flourish and found many references to the word in Psalms. In Psalm 92:1 it reads, "The righteous will flourish like a palm tree, they will grow like a cedar of Lebanon." Or in Psalm 52:8 "But I am like an Olive tree flourishing in the house of God; I trust in God's unfailing love for ever and ever." There are several other verses that use the metaphors of our being like a flourishing tree or plant without using the term flouring but it is implied, (Psalm 1:3; Psalm 144:12; Proverbs 11:28; Jeremiah 17:8).

Metaphors are powerful to learn from. The scriptures look at God's desire for us not as shriveled up plants or dried up dead trees. The verses mentioned above describes God's people as flourishing, healthy trees. Of course this is a metaphor, not that we become real trees even though some agnostics and atheists writers I have read often think those like myself, who believe in God, must have a chunk of wood for a brain. But back to the metaphor, the Bible describes us as trees that are so strong they can withstand strong winds and storms and are fruitful as well. The metaphor carries with it that our lives are to be positive and have meaning in being fruitful so that we have a purpose in our daily living. So, that we are strong to meet the challenges and storms of each day. This is what I appreciate about Positive Psychology is that it's focus is on making people stronger and more fruitful in their life.

Observations of people also shaped my thinking. I have always enjoyed observing people in life. In the first chapter where I look at our common problem in this life journey I mention my observations that have shaped my thinking. All my observations of people drew me to the I thought is that all there is to life? For example viewing high schoolers high on drugs. With their deadened red eyes and stupored speech I would think what is so great about marijuana? They look and sound stupid! Can't there be more for people to enjoy life more fully? How can people move beyond just existing and live the best life possible?

My belief is people want more than just existing. The movie *It's A Wonderful Life,* has been a popular Christmas classic because people can relate to the message. We want a wonderful life but have to deal with all the struggles that come into our journey. I doubt people would have turned the movie into a classic if it was called "It's a

Terrible Life". We want the positive in our lives not the negatives. Even the chronic complainers among us are complaining because they want a better life. We want a life more than just getting along. That is what Living More than OK is all about.

Before we as a family made a move to a new location in Texas, a co-worker of my wife, bought her three wooden sea gulls. On the wooden base each bird was attached the words "Live, Love, Laugh". We placed them in our new house in a built-in display shelf as one enters the living room area.

These three words capture much of the spirit of Positive Psychology in living our lives more than ok. After the move as we walked through our neighborhood I noticed a couple houses have decorative signs with the saying "Live, Love, Laugh". I became curious what the background of this new popular phrase of these three words. As I searched about these words on the internet I saw one sign that expands on them "Live Well, Love Much, Laugh Often". Wondering about the background of this phrase I then searched where the phrase came from. A website stated that the phrase came from a poem by a poetess, Bessie Anderson Stanley. Here is a copy of the poem.

Bessie Anderson Stanley wrote a poem in 1904 entitled "Success." It reads in its entirety:

He has achieved success who has lived well, laughed often, and loved much;
Who has enjoyed the trust of pure women, the respect of intelligent men and the love of little children;
Who has filled his niche and accomplished his task;
Who has never lacked appreciation of Earth's beauty or failed to express it;
Who has left the world better than he found it,
Whether an improved poppy, a perfect poem, or a rescued soul;
Who has always looked for the best in others and given them the best he had;
Whose life was an inspiration;
Whose memory a benediction.

Let's look at each word the first being "Live". We are placed on this earth to live not boring lives but to live well. We need to make the most of life and enjoy our time to the fullest. From the text of the poem the "live" is not just selfish existence but to make the world a better place. Take time to enjoy the beauty of creation. Living is also relating in a way to others to build them up. I see in the poem the importance of mentoring people around us to bring out the best in them.

The second word in the sequence in our bird picture is "Love". In the poem the thought is to love much. The first thought that comes to my mind is the Greek term agape the one word for love that is used in the Greek New Testament in the context of God's unconditional love. Also sacrificial love as is described in the Love chapter of the Bible, I Corinthians 13. Here is an except from verses 1–7:

If I speak in the tongues[a] of men or of angels, but do not have love, I am only a resounding gong or a clanging cymbal. 2 If I have the gift of prophecy and can fathom all mysteries and all knowledge, and if I have a faith that can move mountains, but do not have love, I am nothing. 3 If I give all I possess to the poor and give over my body to hardship that I may boast,[b] but do not have love, I gain nothing.

4 Love is patient, love is kind. It does not envy, it does not boast, it is not proud. 5 It does not dishonor others, it is not self-seeking, it is not easily angered, it keeps no record of wrongs. 6 Love does not delight in evil but rejoices with the truth. 7 It always protects, always trusts, always hopes, always perseveres.

This love lived out in our lives can as the poem says, help us be a person who "left the world better than he found it . . .".

The third word is laugh. The poem speaks of laughing often. A verse from Proverbs comes to mind. Proverbs 17:22 "*A joyful heart is good medicine, but a crushed spirit dries up the bones.*" Laughter brings joy to our life and heart. Laughter is good therapy to help us be healthy as it relaxes us. It is a natural stress reliever. Comedy films are often popular as they help people feel good afterwards. Laughter therefore helps us to live better. It can brighten up a dreary boring day. Laughter also helps us from taking ourselves and life too seriously. I am all for being serious about life but sometimes we go overboard and we then need to learn to laugh at ourselves.

So as you read through this book you will see that many of the principles I share with you will focus in on living well. One question to keep in mind as you read through the chapters is are you Living Well, Loving Much, and Laughing Often?

At the end of the first chapter I mentioned, I enjoy listening to all kinds of music. There is power in the music itself and also power in thinking through the lyrics. So in this book you will see a song listed with its lyrics in most chapters. The purpose is for you to think through the issue of each chapter from a music point of view. As I mentioned earlier simply search on the internet with your nearby electronic device the title of the song and you will find a variety of videos that relate to the songs I mention.

For this second chapter I have chosen a song *More than Fine* by the Band Switchfoot. I still remember the one semester I had a student, named Heath, (more of his story later), brought me a CD of the band Switchfoot and said, "Sir, you have to listen to this band." Their song *More Than Fine*, I felt had some important thoughts to ponder about life and how to live to the fullest—the importance of Living More Than OK. I will just share a few of my thoughts about this song this student brought into my life. Again I encourage you to look it up online for more personal reflection on the lyrics.

The lyrics point out to me an exciting way to look at life. It challenges me to consider what am I putting into my life to enjoy a better life for myself and my family. Living with expanded possibilities for the potential we have is like looking out at the vastness of the ocean. If you have been to any large body of water you can picture what the song is saying "more than oceans away from who we are . . .". I remember gazing off into the Pacific Ocean from the beaches in Hawaii and on the beaches of the west coast. The water seems to go on forever That is how our possibilities in life can be if we are open to living beyond existing. Reflect over how our impact in the world can be if we are open to living more than ok.

There is a phrase in the song "I want to blow into pieces" reminds me of a quote "people are like sticks of dynamite, the power is on the inside . . . but nothing happens until the fuse is lit." from a book by Mac Anderson in his *Attitude is Powerful.* There is so much powerful potential in each of us. The problem is we need to light the fuse.

Not settling for the mundane of getting by, but blasting off beyond the blue skies. How many of us blast out of bed in the morning looking at the opportunities we have to serve and grow. Instead we cover our heads and hit the snooze button hoping the day disappears. How many of us give up on our dreams or are not open to new dreams for our lives? We settle for what we begin to think is fine when there is so much more potential out in the vastness of the ocean of life for better present situations and futures. My desire with this book is to send out ideas and thoughts to help you move beyond the boredom of ok and getting by—to blasting out in the possibilities of life. Don't give up or back down in your life!

Reflection:

Are you just in existence mode in your present life journey?

What are some possibilities do you see in the ocean of life to improve your life and future?

List some of the major turning points in your life journey that have made you want to make more of your life.

Reflect over the three words Live, Love, Laugh. What do they mean to you? Think over the poem and ask yourself

how can you be an inspiration this week? On the coming weekend rent a comedy movie and enjoy some laughs.

If you were a tree what kind of tree would you be? Thinking of the three core features of Positive Psychology where are you at presently:

What is your level of happiness?

Are you learning something new and excited about it?

What do you see as your primary purpose in life at the present time?

Resources for further growth:

Anderson, Mac, The Power of Attitude, Thomas Nelson, 2004.
Ben-Shahar, Tal Happier, McGraw-Hill, 2007 (Check out his website for other positive life thoughts—http://www.talbenshahar.com).
Seligman, Martin, Authentic Happiness, Free Press, 2002.
Seligman, Martin, Flourish, Free Press, 2011.
Switchfoot, "More Than Fine" Beautiful Letdown CD. 2003.

The Importance of
Becoming A Bookhead

Why have a chapter on reading in a book on Positive Psychology? Also what is a Bookhead? You will not find reading as a topic within positive psychology so why a chapter on it? First of all again it is my book, so if I feel reading is important therefore, I am putting it in. There—case closed—hope you keep reading! I deeply feel an important element to Living a More Than OK life is reading. It is distressing to me to see in today's world reading has seen an enormous decline. I observe this in College students in my classes where fewer say they enjoy reading. Many try to get by in their classes with the least amount of reading as possible. Also news reports have shown the populace is reading less and less. Even if there are fewer people reading that does not negate the importance of it. Reading helps in expanding our minds to learn new ideas and practical information for our lives. Reading is one primary way we learn in our education.

I place reading here early in the book as reading had a major impact in my life. Early on in my life my mother, starting when I was in second grade each Summer enrolled me in our town's library reading program. Each year from then on I was hooked with reading. I participated in the Summer library reading program each year until I went into Jr. High. By then it was such a habit, reading became one of my favorite pastime activities. My first job was in my hometown library while I was attending High School.

Back in second grade due to life problems in my family, I was considered slow in school. Reading changed that as it helped with my vocabulary and I had to tell the librarian what I read so that helped improve my communication. I read fiction and that helped with my imagination and creativity. In third grade I had the most influential teacher in my life, Mrs. Verna Clifford. Reading and writing stories were a big part of her teaching program with us. I had been extremely introverted due to early stressors of my father dying when I was two years old. In response to his death I withdrew emotionally so started school a year later than I should have. My extreme shyness and quietness caused the school system to me labels as slow. Mrs. Clifford helped again by encouraging reading to improve my test scores so that I was not labeled "a slow learner". I believe the reading was a major element in my improvement. So personally I saw the change reading brought for me so I see the importance in helping improve the mind through reading.

This came close to home when I was trying to encourage our adopted young teen daughter to read more books when she had first come into our lives. She had what I thought was an interesting argument for me to consider. She told me that she was not a "Bookhead like me." I immediately thought of the full bookshelves in my home office and the two full bookshelves in my work office. Bookhead—I liked the term. So I became Mr. Bookhead. I reminded her she did not have to be a Bookhead but would need to remember reading is important to do well in school and life. So I thank my daughter for bring the term Bookhead into my life.

To me being a Bookhead is being a lover of books and reading. Reading is a way to expand your mind and make your life more than ok. Fiction books can take you places in your mind that may encourage you to travel or try out something new in your life. Or just the imagination side of fiction can bring fulfilling enjoyment to a boring day. Nonfiction books provide knowledge to grow your mind and explore new experiences in life. They also help build critical thinking skills as you think through ideas and issues in nonfiction books.

There have been studies in the recent years showing a decline in reading. The *National Endowments for the Arts* did a study on the decline in reading from 1982–2002. Any drop in reading levels or people who think reading is boring makes me want to shout out the positive side of building a habit of reading in our lives. In an era where the news points to a decline in reading I would like to encourage you to try out being a Bookhead as one way to improve your life.

In the book, *This Unbearable Boredom of Being*, the author, Genrich Krasko, speaks of the importance of reading—"But one cannot build up one's personality, with high self esteem and a mature approach to life without reading and reading a lot. Extinction of books will eventually bring about the extinction of Western Civilization." Reading a wide selection of books will build our lives up with stronger minds and deeper fulfillment. Support your local library and local bookstores by making a commitment to watch less TV, less internet surfing, (unless you are reading informative blogs such as mine), and make time to read more books. Start with topics and reading styles you enjoy and branch out from there. For encouraging younger people to read check out the website, http:// www.readkiddoread.com/home by author James Patterson. It is a helpful resource for encouraging young people to read. I like how James Patterson goes out of his way to support reading in young people. One key in moving beyond ok in your life is by becoming a Bookhead—find what books you enjoy and enjoy a relaxing, fulfilling reading time in your schedule!

Part of the importance of this chapter is to promote reading. I do understand that part of the struggle in today's world there are many things that pull people's time from reading. Sometimes it seems like a battle to convince students they need to make reading a priority. One recent book I finished gave me a disconcerting feeling about the state to reading in society. As I read the book by author Mark Bauerlein, a Professor of English at Emory University, I knew he is so right, even though I wish he wasn't.

The book is *The Dumbest Generation: How the Digital Age Stupefies Young Americans and Jeopardizes Our Future*. The author presents the case of how the decline in reading is detrimental to our youth and maybe the future of our country. Many studies are presented that reveal the decline of reading in all age groups in America with a special focus on the youth population. The hardest part for me was the statements listed by educators saying it is ok that the youth are not enjoying reading but rather mindlessly texting, playing videos, and absorbed in Facebook. He mentions at one of his presentations on his research on Reading at Risk, a Professor of Renaissance Literature spoke out, "I don't care if everybody stops reading Literature. Yeah, it's my bread and butter, but cultures change. People do different things." (page 60). How can an educated person say such a thing??! Reading is so important in developing the mind and thinking skills. A Literature Professor should be helping encourage students to read instead of encouraging mindless activities that take the place of reading.

I highly recommend the book if you have not read it, even though I mentioned it gave me an uneasy feeling. It is sad to know the importance of reading in the development of the mind and then read of the research that shows young people spend so little time reading and often say it is boring. Yes it can seem boring when compared to the sights and sounds of YouTube videos and video games. If they could only see how reading fiction stories can tap into the creative part of the mind as you imagine the scenes being described on the pages. I am not the type to say people should stay away for the internet or computer games. There are many fine features to these tools for self improvement of the mind. But reading should be held up as an enjoyable and important way to grow our minds.

During my over ten years of working with University students I have seen what Professor Bauerlein in saying. It is a rarity to see students reading on campus or before class. When I was in college I would use my spare time to read. In my Divinity School for my first Master's degree, one Professor encouraged us to read a non-class book once a month. Or course I was and am a bookhead so it would be more natural for me to be reading. Also back then you did not have a laptop always, so as to surf mindless information on the internet. I say mindless not to say all the internet is mindless as there are educational elements to websites. But for example go to the Youtube homepage. Are there usually any videos that promote culture and higher values on their main page? No they are usually mind numbing wastes of time. As one day in the news they mentioned a video going "Viral" of a newswoman being hit in the head by a soccer ball. How is watching a video of seeing a lady get hit in the head by a ball uplifting to the human spirit? Or consider all the brainless videos of cats and babies dancing! That is uplifting? Positive? A good use of computer viewing time? I don't believe so and I doubt anyone can come up with a rational defense of spending hours looking at such things to better one's life.

One positive change idea Bauerlein brings up is found in this passage of the book, "Young people need mentors not to go with the youth flow, but to stand staunchly against it, to represent something smarter and finer than the cacophony of social life. They don't need more pop culture and youth perspectives in the classroom. They get enough of those on their own. Young Americans need someone somewhere in their lives to reveal to them bigger and better stories than the sagas of summer parties and dormitory diversions and Facebook sites." (page 199) We need to have those of us who enjoy reading and know of its importance to better our lives to promote the cause. I would love to see Professor Bauerlein write another book Changing the Dumbest Generation to the Best Generation using practical ideas on how we can stem the tide in reading.

As I stated I have seen what the Professor is speaking of in my interaction with students as a career counselor and teacher of a freshman success class. Usually the students I see that are excelling are the few that I will see with a fiction book or they mention they enjoy reading, I know this is just anecdotal evidence from my observations. Matter of fact that would be a useful research project for the future. Do research on students on both extremes of the academic spectrum; those who excel in their classes and those who do poorly in college, and compare their reading habits. I would assume those who do well would have higher scoring of interest in reading.

I am thankful as I stated before my mother saw the importance of reading in having me be involved with reading clubs at our city library when I was in elementary school. That helped shape me as a bookhead early on.

Here are a few websites that help promote reading:

www.adlit.org/article/19793
www.wnba-books.org/
charityguide.org/volunteer/fifteen/reading-books.htm

Books, whether fiction or non-fiction, are expressions of ideas, concepts, facts, and stories. These ideas can have a positive impact on our mental attitude in our inner programming. Working with students I have seen the power of stories in getting ideas across to them. One of the stories I tell college students when discussing the subject of all the reading they will need to do in their lives is the story of Dr. Ben Carson. His is an amazing story of how reading can change a life. He tells in his autobiography, *Gifted Hands*, of how he always struggled in school and felt he was a dummy. But his mother who believed in him made he and his brother to read and write book reports to her each week. This forced reading was the building block that changed his life as he saw himself doing better in school because of it. He went on to graduate with honors and eventually became a neurosurgeon at John Hopkins Hospital. His story shows the power of reading to change lives. His story is a book that should be given to every young person to see how reading is important.

Building a habit of reading is important in keeping the mind active and growing. Your reading can be a positive influence on your mental attitude. Beginning with reading topics of interest, helps in understanding and gaining new insights in your areas you enjoy. No matter how good we think we are in a certain area there is always room for improvement. When I do classroom assessments that have a rating scale 1-10 I remind students never give themselves a 10 as there is always room to grow during our journey in this life.

Reading about new topics may open new ideas to your life or challenge your viewpoints. By challenging our thinking we can think through and confirm on a deeper level what we believe and why we believe it. Read material from opposing points of view as that helps understand where others are coming from in their emotions and logic, (or lack of logic), on particular areas. Looking at life as a Christian, I have read Bertrand Russell, Sam Harris, Christopher Hitchens, and Eric Maisel's works promoting atheism. Reading their works has actually helps bolster my faith. Their arguments did not win me over and in certain cases their hatred for those who believe in a religious Worldview turned me off.

Magazines and newspapers are reading materials that offer news reporting and information on a wide variety of topics on a smaller scale than books. Reading these are a great way to keep informed on what is going on in the world. As with books if you have a personal area of interest, like flowers, traveling, cars, or cooking find a magazine related to your interest. If magazine subscriptions are too costly an idea is to put in your weekly schedule a time period to visit your local library and relax and read in their magazine room.

Once a student in my Student Success class mentioned to me that he did not like reading books but he researched a lot of his interests about computer networking and news information on the internet. He asked me if that was ok. We live in a computer and internet world. He had a deep passion for computers and I knew he devoured information off the internet. I mentioned to him and the class that there is a lot of bad on the internet but also a lot of good, (like my blog!). In thinking of our reading as part of our mental self-talk programming be questioning of any source be it paper or cyber based. Glean out the positives that will help you improve where you are going in your life journey.

I know electronic books are becoming more popular but I believe I will always be a hard copy book person. To me there is nothing like sitting at my desk turning the actual pages of a book as I read. Likewise, searching for books at a library or bookstore, being able to pull the book off a shelf and leaf through it, is much more satisfying than viewing a virtual image on a computer screen where you can only look at the two pages the publisher allows you to look at.

In closing this chapter I am not telling you to be a Bookhead like me. Would I like to see that? Yes a better world would be a Bookhead world in my opinion. But that is all it is my opinion. As I previously mentioned we are all different. What I do want to get across to you is that no matter what your interests are do make time for reading for the continued growth of your mind and personal life.

Reflection:

Do you take time in your schedule for reading? Reflect over why reading is important to you? Think over how you can promote reading to those around you.

Here is my list of ten favorite influential books in my personal life, (outside of the Bible which is a regular source of reading in my life):

1. *Mere Christianity*, C.S. Lewis http://www.cslewis.org/
2. *The Road Less Traveled*, M. Scott Peck, M.D. http://www.mscottpeck.com/
3. *What's So Amazing About Grace?* Philip Yancey, http://www.philipyancey.com/
4. *Who Are You Really And What Do You Really Want?* Shad Helmstetter Ph. D. http://www.shadhelmstetter.com/
5. *Choice Theory*, William Glasser http://www.wglasser.com/
6. *Man's Search For Meaning*, Victor Frankl http://www.viktorfrankl.org/e/indexe.html
7. *What Color is Your Parachute?* Richard Bolles http://www.jobhuntersbible.com/
8. *The Success Journey*, John Maxwell (now titled *Your Roadmap For Success*) http://www.johnmaxwell.com/
9. *Flourish, Martin Seligman* http://www.billohanlon.com/

10. *Critical Thinking: Tools for Taking Charge of Your Professional and Personal Life*, Richard W. Paul and Linda Elder http://www.criticalthinking.org/

Think over the books you have read. Which are books that have been influential in your life? Have they positively helped in your positive mental programming?

References for further learning

Reading in decline—http://www.nea.gov/news/news04/readingatrisk.html
Bauerlein, Mark, The Dumbest Generation, Penguin, 2009
Carson, Ben, Gifted Hands, Zondervan, 1990
Krasko, Genrich, This Unbearable Boredom of Being, I Universe Inc. 2004

***I am a working on another book on the joy and importance of reading. I would appreciate your personal thoughts on the questions below. Simply email me your thoughts to me at livingmorethanok@gmail.com Place I love books in the subject line.

1. Why do you think reading is important?
2. Is there a particular book that has had special impact and meaning to you?

Thank you for your help!
Frank Coulson M. Ed., M. Div., LPC, NCC
Check out my Personal Growth Blog:
www.livingmorethanok.blogspot.com

Living More Than OK
Using Critical Thinking

From the time we wake up in the morning and debate hitting the snooze button we are thinking thoughts that are constantly flooding our mind. It could be said even during our sleep the mind is active during our dreams states. How do these thoughts affect our living? Is just ok living affected by just ok thinking? By improving our thinking skills can we move beyond ok to abundant living? That is what I would like to challenge you about your thinking in this chapter. How critical thinking can improve our living?

What is Critical Thinking? One of my favorite definitions of it comes from Richard Paul, one of the top researchers and writers about critical thinking. He states, "Critical Thinking is thinking about your thinking while you are thinking, in order to make your thinking better." That is a lot of thinking! A longer more descriptive definition from Richard Paul and Michael Scrivin is "Critical thinking is the intellectually disciplined process of actively and skillfully conceptualizing, applying, analyzing, synthesizing, and/or evaluating information gathered from, or generated by, observation, experience, reflection, reasoning, or communication, as a guide to belief and action. In its exemplary form, it is based on universal intellectual values that transcend subject matter divisions: clarity, accuracy, precision, consistency, relevance, sound evidence, good reasons, depth, breadth, and fairness". To me it means to actively reflect over your thinking analyzing and looking at the logic to improve your thought life. I tell my college students I work with that the brain is like a computer and our thinking is like the software programs. Critical thinking is studying over our program of thoughts with the motive to improve our amazing personal computer in our head.

The important question is what is the quality of our thinking? Have you ever watched a news story and said to your self—"What were they thinking?". There are examples of bad thinking all over the media. When I want to get a good laugh out of poor quality thinking I check out Chuck Shepherd's website News of the Weird. It is also a column found in several local weekly community papers. I can laugh at the antics of the results of people's thinking yet the problem is when I catch myself saying, "what was I thinking?" Those moments are when I especially understand the need for critical thinking—analyzing my thinking to improve it.

Those who write about critical thinking take care to note that it is the lack of sound thinking that causes much of our personal problems and societal problems. Often the problem is that people just don't think, they just react without actively thinking. They live with their brain on autopilot. The best description on those who do not use critical thinking came to my mind once, when I was listening to the Rush Limbaugh show while driving. He was talking about people who blindly follow ideology as "mind numbed robots". I thought that was an excellent picture. Their thought patterns seem totally blank and they just mechanically respond to what they are told by their ideology without thinking it through. Many do not like Rush Limbaugh and I do not religiously follow his program. Yet I must say I have been very impressed over the years when I do hear him he often laments the lack of critical thinking in our society. He also encourages people to think for themselves not just follow what he is saying.

One concern on bringing up the issue of critical thinking is how the lack of it affects our personal lives in negative ways, but the lack of it can even be seen on a national level as well. The most telling example of this in my opinion is what I viewed with the Benghazi massacre that occurred September 11th, 2012. Four brave Americans were killed in the Benghazi, Libya diplomatic compound. It was close to the presidential election and immediately

President Obama and his staff were saying it was all the fault of a YouTube video? I immediately questioned this in my mind. But the left leaning main stream media ran with the story from the Obama team. Fox News was the only outlet to initially take a critical look at the tragedy and question the administration. Libya's own ruler came out and said it was a terrorist attack within a day or two, yet the Obama protecting media kept supporting the lie and cover up of Obama and Hilary Clinton continual blame game of the YouTube video. Was there outrage among the people of America? No they simply unquestioningly listened to the Obama controlled media and thought it was the YouTube video and went back to their mind-numbing watching of reality TV shows. For weeks and months the Obama team emphasized that it was the YouTube video even placing the creator of it in prison when all the facts pointed to a terrorist attack.

Why it bothered me so, is at that time, I immediately thought back to growing up and being in Ohio in 1970 as a young teen when the Kent State University massacre occurred. Four students were killed on the campus and it caused a shift in the nation's thinking about the Vietnam War. There was even a song "4 Dead In Ohio" that became an anti-war song. Watching the coverage of the Benghazi cover-up and lies from Obama and his staff I thought, where was the song for the four brave men who died there? Why was there no cry from the citizenry? Could it be because the ability to critically think has gone down since the 1970's? One of the shames of the Benghazi mess to me is that if the cover-up was to protect Obama's re-election, he probably would have won even by a larger margin if he would have been a real leader and sought to help the four men and the many others who were injured in the attack.

Two authors that have spoken so well to the issue of critical thinking over the years are Richard Paul and Linda Elder. One of my favorite books on critical thinking is their *Critical Thinking: Tools For Taking Charge of Your Professional Life and Personal Life*. In their writing they point out that three main functions of the mind are thinking, (comparing, judging, analyzing and synthesizing); Feeling, (happy, sad, depressed, calm, and worried); and wanting, (goals, purposes, values, and motives). Each waking moment our minds are thinking through these areas as we relate to life and our environment. Our thoughts are moving either passively or actively. Critical thinking comes to play as we take the active control of our thoughts. Our thoughts either control us passively by emotionally responding, or we control our thoughts by actively rationally, "thinking about our thinking".

Our life is about the choices we make in our decision process. With each choice there is a consequence and then we make another decision based on that consequence and so on. If we are not critically thinking life happens to us—sometimes with bad consequences. Maybe even to the level of being in a news story where others look at us and say, "what was he thinking?". Hopefully not to the level that we appear in News of the Weird! By actively using critical thinking we can have more control over our living, make more positive choices that will bring better results in our lives. That is why I believe critical thinking is so important in Living More Than OK.

Of course we can't control everything just by our thinking. Using critical thinking won't stop a storm from destroying our house or from a illness coming into our life. It won't stop the affects of other people's poor quality thinking, whether they are family, friends, or politicians from affecting our personal lives. Do know that the habit of building stronger thinking patterns will help you respond positively and constructively to events and actions that come into our life journey.

We all can develop our critical thinking skills and this will help in our Living More Than OK. There are personality theories that bring up the point that some people are more predisposed to be thinkers while others may be more of doers for example. When we look at those around us we do notice differences in people's thinking. Some people jump right into different activities or relationships while others think through deeply before they make a move. This just shows we are different and unique. Our thinking skills fall on a continuum and on that continuum we can always rise to a higher level. We can always grow stronger in our thinking abilities. The important point is that we can all improve our critical thinking skills which will help in every aspect of life, personal relationships, money matters, health, work, future plans, and etc.

Remember that critical thinking is not a negative activity of putting things down or having a negative cranky spirit. Vincent Ruggiero in his book *Making Your Mind Matter,* shows that critical thinking is a positive activity of evaluating ideas from others and yourself in order to improve the ideas and choose the best one. This relates well as I previously mentioned Richard Paul and Linda Elder in their writings bring out that questioning is key to critical thinking. Ruggiero in his book, mentions a thinking style which I feel captures important features of critical thinking as it relates to daily challenges we all face. He calls it the **WISE** approach. This is one way in which to improve critical thinking in our life.

Wonder—Go through each day with a sense of wonder making note and observations of your experience and thoughts during the day. You may want to record key events problems, and thoughts relevant in a journal.

Investigate—With key problems or important issues do thoughtful research for solutions.

Speculate—Use the power of questions in relation to problems and life issues. Brainstorm creative solutions.

Evaluate—Try out the solutions to challenges you face during the day and look for the most effective ways to improve your life.

Another way to improve our thinking is Richard Paul and Linda Elder's admonition that we should become a critic of our own thinking. Again this is not a negative hitting ourselves on the head, "Oh, I'm so stupid. I just can't think!" No it is taking the time to "think about your thinking in order to make it better". Take some time to ponder over your thinking, how do you think through issues facing you? What have been the circumstances that resulted from your thinking? How can you improve your thinking quality.

The being a critic of our thinking approach reminds me of a verse in the Apostle Paul's writing *2 Corinthians 10:5 (NIV) ". . . and we take captive every thought to make it obedient to Christ."* He is looking at our thought life from the spiritual standpoint of actively taking charge and control of our thoughts instead of drifting through our mental life on autopilot. The principle relates to all aspects of thought to be in control of our thinking and actively have our thoughts captive so we know why we believe what we believe and understand the thought process behind our actions.

Another important way to improve our thinking is as I mentioned in the previous chapter is to be a Bookhead. Read up on how to improve your thinking. We need to be life long learners. Here are a few book recommendations:

Critical Thinking—Tools for Taking Charge of Your Professional and Personal Life by Richard Paul & Linda Elder.

Thinking For a Change by John Maxwell. (Love that title!)

Making Your Mind Matter by Vincent Ruggiero

25 Days to Better Thinking & Better Living by Dr. Linda Elder & Dr. Richard Paul (This is a short book where you can devote a day at a time for 25 days on different aspects of improving your thinking.)

Also make use of Internet resources to improve your knowledge of critical thinking:

www.criticalthinking.org This website has numerous resource articles to expand your thinking on Critical Thinking.

http://www.rebtnetwork.org/whatis.html This is a website about Albert Ellis' Rational Emotive Behavior Therapy (REBT). His theory helps us see the need for critical thinking as many of our problems are based in our faulty beliefs. There are very helpful ideas on this website to help improve our thinking process. Much of psychology in the Cognitive Behavioral school of thought focuses in on the quality of our thinking.

In thinking about our thinking negative vs. positive thoughts are something we need to consider. If you ponder about your thought life you may find you think more negative thoughts than positive. I have noticed when I talk to college students about feelings and ask for names of feelings often the first 6 or 7 feelings stated will be negative in nature—sadness, hate, envy, . . . If you find you come up with more negatives, don't start feeling too bad. Dr. Shad Helmstetter in his book, *Who Are You Really and What Do You Want?* states there is some research that shows for some people up to 70% of their thinking is negative. That is a big chunk of negativity. What can we do to change the percentages in a positive direction?

One key area where we can improve our thinking in a more positive way is what we say to ourselves—our self talk. Yes it is ok to talk to yourself. We do it all the time. You probably don't want to walk through the shopping mall holding a long dialogue with yourself. You will get a lot of strange looks but seriously, it is important to consider the things we say to ourselves.

I remember years ago in a College basic computer programming class learning the acronym, GIGO, Garbage In Garbage Out. The professor mentioned that it applies to how computer programs are written but he also stated to use it for our own thought life. If your computer program of your thoughts and self-talk is filled with errors, your output on the program will be filled with errors. The professor mentioned that in his opinion the greatest computer ever designed was the human brain designed by God. He exhorted the class to apply the GIGO principle to our lives and thinking. If you allow garbage in to your minds the output into your life will be garbage. Again this goes back to critical thinking of thinking about your thinking.

While I was studying on my first Masters degree in Divinity/ Counseling at Trinity Evangelical Divinity School in Deerfield, IL my advisor encouraged me to read the Dr. Helmstetter book, *What To Say When You Talk To Yourself*. This, along with my appreciation for Cognitive Behavioral theories in my Psychology courses caused me to be awestruck by the power of our thinking in our individual lives.

Examples of Self-talk is the internal scripts we say to ourselves in our minds—"Boy, I'm sure having a rotten day!", "How could I be so stupid", "I should be able to do this better", "I will never be able to remember things!", "My mom said I would always be a failure. I guess she was right." "I just can't be creative!". The scripts are programming statements that we consciously and unconsciously repeat over and over to ourselves. These statements program our personal internal computer, (our brain). When the programming is full of shoulds, coulds, can'ts and regrets; we are programming major negativity which will produce negativity in our lives.

When I first read Dr. Helmstetter's, I reflected over all the "I can't" statements that had limited my past from my teen years and negatively affected the present at the time while I was studying for my first graduate degree. I was astounded at the negativity and limitations I had placed on myself, almost unknowingly. I would like to say that that realization changed my life to success over night. Mental habits are slow in changing. Even up to this day. Before starting my blog for months I remember arguing with myself, *"Why bother writing a blog you have nothing to say. You can't do it. Who will read it anyways? It won't help anyone"* I finally reprogrammed my self talk with *"I have always wanted to work on improving my writing. Doing a blog may be productive writing practice. Even if I only get a few readers, if I can encourage them to live a more than ok existence it will be worth it."* I have had the same mental negativity in working on this book. "Who am I to write a book? Who will bother to read it? I have changed my thinking to believe the positive psychology principles I am trying to get across will be helpful to those who read so even if just a few people can live a more than OK life from reading this book it will be worth it.

In this paragraph I give an example of the primary way Dr. Helmstetter promotes to change the thinking programs in our minds. Set aside 30 minutes of quiet alone time to think over your self-talk statements you say to yourself on a routine basis. Jot down on a paper the things you say to yourself—Examples—"Why me?"; "I never say the right thing"; "my room is always messy—I guess I am just a messy person"; "nobody likes me"; "I just can't lose weight". Look over the statements. Are they things you really want to be true about yourself? Can you have pride in saying these things? Are they helping you to be a better person? Then finally think over what you should be saying instead and write the new programming statements out. Here are some examples—change the "I can't" to "I can"; "I am having a rotten day nothing is going right" to "My day is starting off rough but I am not going to let it beat me. Look out world here I come!"; "My dad said I would always be a dummy in math" to "Maybe I am not a numbers guy but I need Algebra to get my degree so I will use the campus tutoring and do extra practice to make sure I pass."

You get the idea. Look at the negative statements you are telling yourself and create a positive new thought program. Then when you catch yourself saying the negative statement hit the delete button in your mind to erase it and then paste in the more positive statement. Try the 30 minute exercise mentioned in the preceding paragraph and try building some new positive programs for yourself. Let your thoughts move your life in a positive direction!

From my Christian worldview in thinking about the importance of our thoughts, a verse in the Old Testament book of Proverbs 23:7 came to my mind. In this verse we find these words, *"As a man thinks in his heart so is he."* This is a powerful proverb if you reflect over its importance. Our thoughts are what shapes the real person inside. Our character, values, behavior, dreams, attitudes are all shaped by our thought life. Our environment and genetic makeup has a part in our development but the driving force of development is our thinking processes. This idea raises the bar on our personal responsibility if we consider the power of our thoughts.

I recently re-read a little leather bound book a friend in Chicago gave me years ago, by the writer James Allen. It is called *As A Man Thinketh* It can be found in some libraries and bookstores. Here is a quote from it:

> *A man's mind may be likened to a garden, which may be intelligently cultivated or allowed to run wild; but whether cultivated or neglected, it must, and will, bring forth. If no useful seeds are put into it, then an abundance of useless weed seeds will fall therein, and will continue to produce their kind.*

> *Every thought seed sown or allowed to fall into the mind, and to take root there, produces its own, blossoming sooner or later into act, and bearing its own fruitage of opportunity and circumstance. Good thoughts bear good fruit, bad thoughts bad fruit.*

His analogy of the mind and life to that of a garden is important in contemplating what kind of life we want to lead. When our family visits Chicago we like to visit Chicago's Botanical Gardens as my wife and I always enjoyed visiting there when we lived in Chicago. You can stroll through acres and acres of well manicured gardens full of flowers not weeds. The various gardens there, are a peaceful setting to appreciate a variety of flowers and plants.

Thinking back to Allen's analogy, how do we want our lives to be? Do we want a life in disarray and a mess or a life of beauty? Deep down we want a life of beauty but moving beyond what we want; we must look at what actually is. We can ask ourselves do I have a life in disarray or a life of beauty? Our thoughts have a major effect on the outcome of our lives. It is our thinking that drives our choices for good or for bad. If we are filling our lives with negative thoughts or dwelling on how boring our lives we are not living more than ok. Weeds of life will quickly overtake our daily experience leaving us in disarray.

The Apostle Paul in the New Testament scriptures states an important point of what the focus of our thinking should be.

In Philippians 4:8&9 he says, *"Finally, brethren,) whatever is true, whatever is honorable, whatever is right, whatever is pure, whatever is lovely, whatever is of good repute, if there is any excellence and if anything worthy of praise, dwell on these things."* The focus of our thoughts should be on positive things. Our thoughts should be seeking truth with the aim for excellence. I enjoy The Message paraphrase, by Eugene Peterson of the same verse *"Summing it all up, friends, I'd say you'll do best by filling your minds and meditating on things true, noble, reputable, authentic, compelling, gracious—the best, not the worst; the beautiful, not the ugly; things to praise, not things to curse.* We need to fill our minds and reflect and ponder those thoughts that are the best and thoughts of beauty. How much more could we improve our lives if we took the time to meditate on true, noble, authentic, and gracious thinking?

What would others think of us if our thoughts appeared above our heads like walking billboards. Would they see noble, gracious thoughts? Or would we be embarrassed by the negatives of unfair judgments, negative putdowns, and personal insecurities? Too often we allow negative thoughts gain control. Relationships falter as we have ungracious thinking about those around us. We limit our potential by having untruthful and ugly thoughts about ourselves. These negative thoughts work out to make our lives ugly like an overgrown weed filled garden not a peaceful garden of beauty.

Take some time at the end of the day to reflect over your thoughts of the day. Make a list of the negatives and the positives found in your thought life. Is your list full of road rage thoughts, complaints, and personal putdowns on yourself? What can you do to change the negatives and build up reputable and authentic beautiful thoughts? We will delve more into what you can do in the next post. Until then, take thought of your thoughts.

One way to improve your critical thinking is to listen and read people who are solid thinkers. Here are some I would suggest

Thomas Sowell: He is an American economist and political philosopher. His books and columns in magazines and the web show a solid logical order to his thinking. He is a good example to follow.

Mark Levin: He is a lawyer, and a conservative commentator. His writings are well researched and well thought out.

Charles Krauthammer: He is a medical doctor and political commentator. He is amazing to listen to as he always has solid logical arguments for what he believes.

David Limbaugh: He is a political commentator whose writings are always well researched, and backs up his arguments with facts. He is the brother of the famous talk radio host Rush Limbaugh.

Rush Limbaugh: He is well known for his talk radio program. What I like about him the times I have heard him, he is often encouraging his listeners to critically think through every issue.

Sean Hannity: Conservative radio and TV talk show host who is dedicated to his values and is firm in his backing up what he says on his shows.

Glenn Beck: Conservative radio and TV talk show host who is very passionate about his beliefs. His books always are well researched and he encourages his listeners to think for themselves.

Ann Coulter: She is a conservative social and political commentator. She is a sharp thinker who most always has facts ready to back up her arguments.

Ravi Zacharias: He is a Christian Apologist for the Christian worldview. He is a very sound thinker and his website is worth checking out—http://www.rzim.org

There are many more people I could suggest but the key is find people who you respect and listen with a questioning mind to what they say. The best examples I have seen of critical thinkers are Independents and Conservatives in their thinking style. A couple of websites where I find the columnists very sound in their thinking are The American Spectator—http://spectator.org and World Net Daily—http://www.wnd.com. Through improved critical thinking you are able to come up with sensible solutions for the problems you face in life. So keep improving your critical thinking habits as it will pay off with being able to Live More Than OK.

Reflection:

Think about your thinking. Are you more active or passive in your thinking? How are you controlling life, rather than letting life control you? Take some time to look over the website www.criticalthinking. org_and see if you can gain some helpful insights for your life. Check out the articles in their library section.

How is your critical thinking? Are you a reactor or do you take time to reflect? Are you an assumer or do you look for the facts? Take some time to reflect over some recent problems that have come into your life and examine what your thinking patterns were like. How can you improve your thinking to be a better problem solver?

Resources for further learning:

Allen, James, As A Man Thinketh can be found in libraries and used bookstores as well as online.

Helmstetter, Shad, Who Are You Really And What Do You Want?, Park Avenue Press, 2003.

Maxwell, John, Thinking For A Change, Warner Books, 2003 (One of my favorite authors. He has a wide variety of books he has authored on success and leadership).

Paul, Richard & Elders, Linda, Critical Thinking: Tolls for Taking Charge of Your Professional and Personal Life, Financial

Times: Prentice Hall, 2002 (Also any book from these two are profitable for personal growth).

Ruggiero, Vincent, *Making Your Mind Matter*, Rowman & Littlefield, 2003.

Tapping Into Your Creativity

In our pursuit of Living More Than OK, which is moving beyond mere boring existence, creativity is important to build into our lives. We tend to think of creativity only in the realm of the Arts: music, painting, poetry, theater and dance. These are important and I encourage people to grow their talents in one or more of these. Yet it is important to remember that creativity has a greater impact in all areas of life. Creativity can be used in solving problems, coming up with new ways to keep relationships fresh and alive, or discovering new ways to enjoy life. It is up to each of us to choose to tap into our creative side.

What does creativity have to do with psychology? This brings me to a book I highly recommend to help you tap into your creativity and improve your creativity. The book is *Your Creative Brain*, by Dr. Shelley Carson, a professor and researcher at Harvard University. In the opening chapter she states, "We are all creative. Creativity is the hallmark human capacity that has allowed us to survive thus far. Our brains are wired to be creative, . . ." This reminds me of the words of creative writing professor, Brenda Euland, ". . . you are all original and talented and need to let it out of yourselves; that is to say you have the creative impulse." We are all creative. I like how Dr. Carson mentions it is the hallmark human capacity. When I visit the zoo I do not see turtles and bears painting murals on their habitat walls. As I visit the monkey area I have never seen one typing out a new fiction novel on its laptop. Creativity is one of the things that separate us from the rest of the animal kingdom.

Dr. Carson in her book helps us to see how expansive creativity can be into all areas of our lives if we are open to tapping into what she calls the CREATES brainsets. In her book she sets forth 7 thought patterns we have in us that relate to creativity in our thinking. Her seven brainsets are:

Connect--Looking for connections between items and ideas to come up with new ideas and solutions.

Reason—Making use of the information you have and analyze and organize it for problem solving.

Envision—Using your imagination to explore the possibilities and answer the "What ifs" that come to mind. This reminds me of possibility thinking.

Absorb—This is opening your mind to new ideas and experiences and savor how these new ideas can shape and form something new and creative.

Transform—Dr. Carson says of this, that it is our tapping into our negative energy and distress we may be feeling. We can then transform the pains of life to solutions for future situations. For me it is reminder that we can choose to remain bitter over pain and hurt or transform and learn to be more empathetic to others going through pain.

Evaluate—This is the critiquing phase of looking at creative ideas and seeing which is best to follow.

Stream—This relates to a concept by a Dr. Mihaly Csikszentmihalyi's concept of flow; where creativity seems to be in oneness with our activity and thinking.

Her book goes into detail of her seven brainsets and gives practical exercises at the end of each chapter you can try out to improve your creativity. That is the important help in this book as she shows we are each wired for creativity and that we each can improve our level of creativity.

I want to just share a couple of important helps from the book to help you in your quest to improve your creativity. Then also this may encourage you to seek out this book at your local library or local bookstore. The first item is that a way to being more creative is to continue in lifelong learning. Be open to studying new topics and ideas. This helps build a broad based foundation of general knowledge for the Connect brainset. Don't be narrowly focused in just one area. Dr. Carson provides examples of great people with broad based life experience. Benjamin Franklin was a writer, philosopher and inventor, John Grisham was a lawyer and now a writer, Leonardo Da Vinci was an inventor and an artist. I remember I had a physics teacher who brought in his cello to class and played for us students. Just recently I heard a jazz combo with a killer upright bass player. I found out his day job was that of a math teacher. So be open to adding creative variety to your ideas and skills.

Then also here are some of her ideas to help improve your creative mood of the absorb brainset: Make a playlist of inspirational songs that help encourage creativity, find a relaxing spot that quiets your mind, (hopefully this is a place linked to nature), Take a walk in a favorite natural setting like a park or beach, or carry a notepad or digital recorder to capture creative ideas you may have.

I hope by now if you started with a "But I am not creative" mindset you have changed your mind. This can be a first step to improve your creativity and help you in Living More Than OK.

Part of the continual journey of Living More than OK is tapping into your creativity. I have said it before and keep telling students that we are all creative to some degree. And that degree of creativity in us can grow and improve. Like all aspects of our living to keep life to the fullest we need to keep progressing and growing on our journey. That is so true in creativity. Know which areas of creativity relate to you, writing, poetry, music, drawing, photography or acting. For initial exploring of creativity expressions that fit you explore on the internet websites that relate to creativity here are a few ideas:

www.creativity-portal.com, websitetips.com/creativity or other sites you find on a web search for creativity. These and other websites can help you explore how to tap into your creativity.

Exploring information like that may give you insight whether you wish to work on writing, music or drawing. Another important help in growing in your creativity is doing it. Make time in your schedule to practice the piano, take photos with your camera or set aside time to write. Is this easy to do? To be honest no. The weeds of activities choke out opportunity to practice the creative arts in our lives. The just getting by, ok life is full of these weeds making our time fill up with unimportant activities that keep us from growing into the more than ok life. The life of flourishing abundance we were meant to live. So we need to in our time schedules do our best to honor our potential possibilities for growth by setting aside time for creativity.

One very important way to grow in our creativity is the being a bookhead approach. Take advantage of the great books on tapping into your creativity. I will look at a variety of authors who are expert writers and their books on writing and the arts are like having a personal mentor beside you. You can learn more about creativity and the various art forms by reading their books.

A great author on the subject of creativity is Eric Maisel, Ph. D. He is a family therapist as his Ph D is in Counseling Psychology. Another aspect of his counseling practice is he is a famous Creativity Coach. He has written fiction and nonfiction books. His nonfiction books focus primarily on the arts and creativity. As an author he speaks to the heart of creativity in all of us. His books are very practical as well, with exercises and activities to do and think over. I have in my book library his *Creativity for Life*; *A Writer's Space*, and *Coaching the Artist Within*. What I like is he speaks to all areas of the arts. Personally I am presently trying to grow in my writing side of my creativity. His books have been an encouragement to me as I try to haltingly progress.

Art is an area of life that adds greatly to the quality of our existence. I have always appreciated art talent in others. I say in others as art is one area I am not talented in. My stick figures look sad. One reason my art grades were so low when I was young was that I could not stand looking at my art so I would often throw it away rather than turn it in to the teacher.

Appreciating art is a different story. One of my favorite past times when I lived in Chicago was to visit the Art Institute of Chicago. I even had a yearly membership. I could spend hours walking through the various collections. In front of some of the major works they had benches were you could sit and soak in the visual expression the artist had created. I enjoyed going over the details in my mind and then expand to the big picture so as to capture the emotion and story the artist was trying to communicate. My trips to the art museum were times to de-stress or times to quiet myself within to think more clearly when I was going through difficult issues. Art has that cathartic value in our inner healing.

Once on a vacation to Niagara Falls I met a gentleman, who was showcasing his mother's artwork. Her name is Polly King. I bought a print entitled "Sacre Coeur" that she had painted in France. It is a picture of a sacred church in Paris. I purchased it as my wife has always wanted to visit Paris and I thought this could be motivation for her to reach her goal someday. Her paintings had such a variety of colors and I could understand why, by a short poem she wrote that was listed on the back of the painting.

God must have loved color very much
–he created so much of it
Vast skies with their ever changing hues
–the silver greys
With their sunsets of
Oranges, pinks and purples
The mountains now green, purple, blue.
The grasses and flowers of limitless colors
And tints
And trees with their stark lines

In plumes of green, pinks and yellows
And now orange, scarlet.
What a wonderful world he has created for us.
–Polly King–

I thought it wonderful that her son was keeping her art story of the beauty of art alive. You can see her art work at www.pollykingart.com

For me, art is gifted people reflecting the beauty of God's creation as can be seen in Polly King's statement above. I understand there are other definitions of art, as some in the post-modern realm feel art is all about shocking people. I will grant they have a point that art can be communication of sometimes shocking issues that need to be addressed. Yet I feel sorry for those that stay focused on the shock value and miss all the beauty God has for us to enjoy so we can flourish in our life journey.

If you have had the urge to be creative in the physical arts of drawing painting, pottery or interested in computer graphics take an art class at a local community college. You can also see if there is a local association of artists that may offer classes in art. Don't take the "I'm no good at art as an excuse not to try" (I am the only one allowed to do that—believe me if you saw my stick drawings you would agree!).

An artwork that comes to my mind is this chapter is "Tapestries" by Joy Wallace an artist in Wisconsin. I bring up this piece as it ties into my love of reading and how reading in integral to creativity. I have had this piece of artwork in my library/office area since I bought it over 15 years ago at an Art Festival in Chicago. It has been an inspiration to me about an important aspect of reading— imagination. It is the first piece of artwork I had ever purchased.

First here is a little about the painter and artist. Joy Wallace started doing art shows of her works in 1970 and as I mentioned she is from Wisconsin. She uses a technique called etching which along with her creativity the technique gives her works of art a magical and mystical feeling. You can find out more about her technique and

view more of her artwork at her website listed here: http://www.
joywallace.com/books.htm The link I have here takes you to her
section on Books. Being the Bookhead I am I could not pass up
taking you to that section. But I encourage you to look at all of her
art in her Gallery section.

Now back to Tapestries and reading. The picture took me back
to my childhood in the Summer Reading program at Barberton
Public Library in Barberton, Ohio my hometown. Starting in third
grade, that was a large part of my Summertime, reading fiction
books in a chair at home. What I liked about fiction is I could
imagine the places in the books and the descriptions in my own
way. In "Tapestries", the artist shows a young boy has been reading
and has fallen asleep. Possibly he is dreaming about the story he was
reading. As the book is falling, a flock of white birds, maybe doves,
are flying out of the pages. Is that what he is dreaming of as well?

The birds flying to me can be a metaphor for freedom. When we
read and grow our imagination this way, we are opening up to learn
to be free in expressing our imagination in new ways. This aspect of
reading helps to improve our creativity. Imagination and creativity
helps keep us sharp minded and feeling alive.

I also notice that in the Tapestry art work, the boy's chair is on a
rumpled tapestry rug, as if it is moving and the chair is tilting. Is
that part of his dream from the book as well, that he will be taking a
magical journey to some unknown world on this soon to be flying
Tapestry? I don't know as I do not know what book he is reading?
But I can imagine can't I?

We need to encourage reading in our own lives and in the lives
of children. I am not movie bashing here as I enjoy a nice Disney
film from time to time, and that is part of creativity and imagining
as well. But in a movie visually everything is all spelled out there
for children and adults. With reading their own imagination gets
to kick in and create what the scene and characters actually look
like. I believe that is lost in movies and mindless TV. In reading a
book our imagination is not passive but actively engaged. It is this

active engagement of the mind's imagination that helps improve our minds I believe creatively as well as critically.

You can also learn to appreciate art by visiting a local art museum or when you are visiting a major city visit one of the major art museums as in Chicago, Dallas or New York City. You may also want to take out a book on art at your local library. Take some quiet time at home to reflect over a collections book of a famous artist and enjoy their talent and the message they have in their paintings.

There are also many resources on the internet to learn more about art. Here is a listing of a few art links you may wish to explore:

http://www.artistsnetwork.com/artistsmagazine
http://www.artistdaily.com
http://www.collegeart.org
http://www.artshow.com/orgs
http://www.artpromote.com/famousartist.shtml

Enjoying artwork can help relax you from the stresses you face each day. Art can help you slow down the pace of your life and build up skills of savoring the good things in life. Artwork can inspire you to reach your dreams and goals. As I mentioned that is one reason I purchased a print of Polly King's work "Sacre Coeur" for my wife's dream of visiting France. Tap into your creativity today!

Poetry is another form of art where we can explore and improve our creative powers. Years ago I attended a workshop at El Rocio Retreat_Center in Mission Texas entitled "Psychology and Poetry: The Road to Creative Understanding". The presenter was *Dr. Ben Wilson*, a retired Professor from Sul Ross University in Texas.

I wanted to see how poetry could be used in helping people work through issues in their lives. I was dreading the activity part as I figured we would need to write a poem and I have never considered myself a poet. It is the same way I look at art. I appreciate art talent and art museums but the max I can do with art is poorly drawn stick figures. So I assumed my poetry would be just as bad.

I went into the session with an attitude of what I could learn. Much of the time was spent reading poems on a variety of topics, forgiveness, anger, love, grief. Then we would discuss the poems discerning their meaning from our point of views. Digging into the meaning and hearing the stories behind the poems revealed a power of the poem to bring out emotion from victims of abuse, those going through loss of a loved one, or the anxiety of making a new move on the life journey. Poetry allows for creating a picture in the mind revealing the depths of emotions a person is dealing with. The therapist can use poetry to help a person get in touch with the emotions they are going through. Then solutions and new plans can develop through that. Of course a person does not need to be in therapy to make use of the power of poetry. From the experience I could see how people who enjoy poetry can use it as a personal tool to keep in touch with their emotions.

The last part of the session was our having to write a poem of something we were facing in our life. I did the poem below which I titled "Getting It Done". I felt it was very simplistic yet is was encouraging to hear that those in the group appreciated it.

Getting It Done by Frank Coulson

For years the dream has been in my mind.
The Problem is getting it done.
Through the fog I see the dim vision.
The Problem is getting it done.
There is even passion in the heart for it.
The Problem is getting it done.
There is work, staying healthy,
Family duties, but more honestly fear.
The Problem is getting it done.

The poem relates to the fact that I was thinking of a couple ideas and things I have been wanting to do. Good ideas that deep inside

I have a passion to do that I keep postponing. This book is an example of one. They are dreams that start to fade as the busyness of life overtakes my time. Many of the busy things that stop us from following up and completing our dreams—projects are good things like our exercise schedule or family time. But they can push the passionate dream items further away into a foggy bog. But as I was writing the poem I thought is it really the duties and tasks in life that keep from working on our dreams? Those things accumulate due to a sense of fear of the dream. Fear of failure, Fear of what others may think. Overcoming the fear is making the choice to press on by turning that dream into a workable goal. Then fit components of the goal into a time schedule to accomplish that dream and make it a reality. So I am presently working on a timeline to complete the one dream I have in my mind.

An English Professor mentioned once to me that to be a good poet you need to read poetry so you may want to pick up a book of poetry from your local library. Or here are a few poetry websites you can check out to appreciate poetry more:

famouspoetsandpoems.com
www.poetryfoundation.org
www.poets.org

Music is the last art form I want to look at as a way of tapping into our creativity. One evening at home I was enjoying the PBS show, Woodsong's Old Time Radio Show. I have always enjoyed folk and bluegrass music and this show and the website www.woodsongs.com specializes in promoting this music genre. The host was emphasizing the importance of music in our lives as a force for good. Music makes us happier. It brings joy in our daily experience which helps us have a more than ok life. Seek out music in your life to bring more joy into your life journey.

As I did a workshop on Test Anxiety on my campus a few years ago, I used music to show also the health benefits of music in relaxing and aiding in overcoming anxiety. Music can also act as a motivator to stimulate us to be active. In the workshop I played a song from a Keiko Matsui CD. Her style is contemporary smooth piano jazz. Her music can be very relaxing to listen to. Her music writing is varied and listening to her CD's over and over I always pick up on new nuances I never heard before. She is one of the most creative pianists I have ever heard.

Even though I played trumpet in High School I always was impressed and enjoyed the saxophone. It can really capture the emotion of the artist playing the saxophone. One of my favorite sax players is Tom Braxton of Texas. He is an amazing player. Watching and hearing him play you can tell he enjoys communicating joy in his songs. When I hear him in concert I can sense how easily he gets into the flow of his songs and works in tandem with his band. We have enjoyed hearing him at the Corpus Christi Jazz Festival over the past years. I also appreciate he has a deep Christian faith and is not afraid to be open about his beliefs. Part of the flow of his music is that he is worshipping while he is playing which adds to the deep emotion of his performances.

I always try to be open to new artists to keep an open expanding creative mind. One evening, we as a family went to a concert locally by the world renown Ahn Trio. They are three sisters from Korea all trained at Julliard. I was a little skeptical at first, as I am not too big of a fan of modern classical music. I prefer the old classics. In their literature they mention that their music is all composed for them by modern composers. I am glad we went. They definitely brought joy into our evening. Their talent and skill on the piano, cello, and violin was breath taking.

I encourage you to try to attend a concert of your favorite music artist or go to a concert of someone new to you. Nothing is better than live music with the sight and sounds. Of course you may say your budget just doesn't allow for that. Then do what my wife and I do sometimes. Put one of your favorite CD's in the stereo and then sit back in a soft recliner with your eyes closed and imagine you are listening in a concert hall.

Also for enjoying live music on a budget watch for local university student programs that are often free or a low cost. We recently enjoyed a wonderful classical guitar concert of high school guitar ensembles and the University's guitar ensembles for only $7.00 knowing that the funds were going for music scholarships. Some towns and cities during the Summers offer free music concerts. The free music festivals are one aspect of Chicago we miss.

Try to incorporate more music into your life and see how more joyful your journey is. Building music in your life will increase your own personal creativity levels as well. Think over who are your favorite musicians. Presently my top 5 are:

1. Phil Keaggy
2. Steven Curtis Chapman
3. Tom Braxton
4. Keiko Matsui
5. Michael Card

The musicians I mentioned are contemporary musicians. We can learn about creativity as well by looking back in history and enjoying musicians of the past. I have always enjoyed classical music and as I write one concert comes to mind. Our family went out to a concert of the music of Ludwig van Beethoven's 8th and 9th Symphonies performed by the San Antonio Symphony orchestra. It was a fine evening of music and a time to enjoy the creativity of the musicians and the creativity of Beethoven the composer.

The orchestra started with the Symphony number 8 which was Beethoven's shortest symphony. During this piece I listened to all the intricate musical details of the movements and began to marvel at Beethoven's creative mind. This sense of marvel increased during the performing of his Symphony number 9 which was his last symphonic work and his most popular through the ages up to the present. It was the first symphonic work to make use of a human chorus. The chorus joins during the 4th movement. The lyrics that were used came from the Poem "Ode To Joy", by Friedrich Schiller and selected excerpts by Beethoven:

Ode To Joy

O friends, no more these sounds! Let us sing more cheerful songs, More full of joy!

Joy, bright spark of divinity, Daughter of Elysium, Fire-inspired we tread Thy sanctuary. Thy magic power re-unites All that custom has divided, All men become brothers, Under the sway of thy gentle wings.

Whoever has created An abiding friendship, Or has won A true and loving wife, All who can call at least one soul theirs, Join our song of praise; But those who cannot must creep tearfully Away from our circle.

All creatures drink of joy At natures breast. Just and unjust Alike taste of her gift; She gave us kisses and the fruit of the vine, A tried friend to the end. Even the worm can feel contentment, And the cherub stands before God!

Gladly, like the heavenly bodies Which He sent on their courses Through the splendor of the firmament; Thus, brothers, you should run your race, like a hero going to victory!

You millions, I embrace you. This kiss is for all the world! Brothers, above the starry canopy There must dwell a loving father.

The symphony was completed in 1824 but in his notebooks it is seen that he was working on the piece from 1811. It is also known that he had wanted to write a musical piece that incorporated Schiller's poem since 1793 when we was 22. The poem celebrates friendships and relationships. There is Joy in strong abiding friendships that we can count on being there with us in our life journey.

Back to my marveling at the creativity of Beethoven, while looking down from the balcony of the Majestic Theater listening to his Symphony number 9. I marveled at the variety in the four movements and how all the lines of music for the different instruments came out of one mind. He had to be able to hear in his mind the differing instrumental voices and the whole of the piece so that it was not just senseless noise. That has always amazed me about composers of orchestra symphonies and choral music. How they can write out the individual parts and when it fits together there is a unified music message expressed is simply amazing.

Another marvel about the piece is, that it is known from history that Beethoven was losing his hearing at this time. Concerning this there is the anecdote that when he was directing the premier of this Symphony number 9 he was completely deaf. So deaf, that when the piece was over he was still directing and a singer had to turn him around to see the crowds cheering as he could not hear them. What is amazing to me about this is his spirit of resilience. He could have given up on this piece by saying, "I can't hear anymore so my love of music is done! I have written enough music so the masses should be happy with that. Poor, poor me as I really did want to do this piece about Schiller's poem but it is impossible now!". Resilience does not give in to impossibilities. This is all just conjecture but maybe since he had a desire since age 22 to do a musical number about Schiller's poem that helped as a driving force of inspiration, when otherwise it would have been natural to just give up composing. Listening to the San Antonio Symphony perform the Symphony number 9 I am glad he did not give up but continued with his creativity.

In trying to find a song that goes with this chapter I thought of this song A song about creativity it is: the *Poem of Your Life*, by Michael Card. Since there were no songs linked to the previous couple of chapters I remind you again, what I am suggesting is take a few moments and search for the song title and view the video online so you can capture a better feeling for the song. There are some amazing videos related with this song.

From the song I pick up that our life is a creative poem and song. Our life poem covers the whole range of our pains and joys. As we live and breath we live life and breath with creativity. It is a song that is in each of us and part of our calling is to sing it out. The songwriter reminds us that we need to be open to the colors the rhythm and the rhyme of each days journey. Through understanding our poem of our life we better understand the meaning and purpose God has for our life. The song reminds me of the Bible verse. Ephesians 2:10 "For we are God's handiwork, created in Christ Jesus to do good works, which God prepared in advance for us to do." We are created for good so our lives have a purpose that we can creatively understand as we take time for personal reflection.

In closing this chapter remember you have creativity within you. As Dr. Carson mentions in her book, "You are wired for creativity". From my worldview as a Christian our creativity is a reflection of the Creator God. Whatever viewpoint you have on the world include creativity into your life.

Reflection:

Take some time to explore the above mentioned websites on creativity. What new ideas about creativity did you learn? What area of art do you want to explore and improve in? Write down what yo learned from the experience.

Take a book of artwork by a famous artist out from your local library or find some artwork online. Spend some time reflecting over the art. Choose one painting to focus on and spend 15 minutes looking at it. In a journal write down what was the artist trying to say in the painting. How did the artwork speak to you in your present situation. Did it help relax you? Did it inspire you in some way?

Read a poem and write out the emotions you see in it and what the meaning of the poem is to you. Then think over an important issue in your life and try to write a poem about it. How does the poem make you think of your life being a poem?

Think over what does music mean to you? Jot down your top 5 music artists. Take some time out of your busy life to sit in a comfortable chair and listen through one of your favorite CD's.

Resources for further learning

Card, Michael, "Poem of Your Life", Poema—CD.
Carson, Shelley, Your Creative Brain, Jossey-bass, 2010.
Michalko, Michael, Thinkertoys, 10 Speed Press, 2006 (Check out his creative thinking website at http://creativethinking.net/WP01_Home.htm).

Making The Most Of Your Time/ Savoring Life

How does time relate to Living More Than OK? Is there a psychology of time? Benjamin Franklin is noted to have said, "Does't thou love life? Then do not squander time, for that is the stuff life is made of.", therefore time relates to all of life. This chapter will not be discussing mere time management of how to do a weekly schedule and the importance of using planners. The focus will be on how to make the best use of our time so we can gain more out of our life journey. Managing our time is important because if we do not manage our time; time will manage us. Too often in our stressful lives that is what is happening. We find that we are being chased by time continually. So as you read this chapter see what ideas will help you improve the quality of your time and how you can improve your managing of the 24 hours you are given every day.

If we wish to live a more than an ok life, one important area in our time management we need to include is time for self improvement. Through self improvement and self renewal we can spiral upwards to Living More Than OK. Too often in our lives the stuff of life snuffs out opportunities to take the time in our schedule to improve ourselves. As we improve ourselves and understand ourselves better we can then manage our time based on our values based priorities.

I like the metaphor in Stephen Covey's 7 *Habits of Highly Effective People,* of his seventh habit which he calls Sharpen the Saw. He looks at Sharpening the Saw as our taking time to improve ourselves in four areas of our lives: Physical, Social, Mental, and

Spiritual. The Saw metaphor reminds us that we develop ourselves as a useful tool in our daily living with our work and interaction with others. Also as I have mentioned in the past we each have a purpose. Saws are purposeful when cutting wood, cutting limbs off trees, or cutting plastic/metal pipes to the correct length. We each need to understand our life purpose.

When our life is dull as a saw, it loses it's effectiveness to fulfill it's purpose. We become overcome with boredom and feel purposeless. The dullness also allows our lives to become out of balance and controlled by the stuff of life. We become stuck on autopilot with too many things happening to us instead of taking control and responsibility ourselves to make life happen for our advantage. The dull saw life is living just ok, getting by and enduring the sense of despair. A saw is not meant to be dull and rusty instead to fulfill its purpose, needs to be shiny and sharp. For maximum living we need to be shiny and sharp. That is what sharpening the saw of our life is about.

Looking at the four areas Covey speaks of the first is the Physical. Ask yourself are you taking time in your week for physical fitness? Three to four times a week you should be in some type of physical activity. As a heart patient I exercise daily. I regularly use the treadmill and elliptical machines for aerobic exercise. My wife and I do a Leslie Sansone Walk at Home_workout several times a week several times a week. Of course find out what works for you, gyms, neighborhood jogging, other dvd exercise programs of your choice. The key is to make exercise a part of your life rituals.

The second area is the Social. As the saying goes, "No man is an island". We all interact with others on a daily basis. That is why emotional intelligence is important. Managing and controlling our emotions to better improve our interactions with family, friends and strangers. Do you make time to improve your relationship connections with the significant people in your lives? Taking time to keep family strong and close relationships strong can keep your saw sharp and effective in your other interactions you face in life.

The third area is Mental. From my previous thoughts on critical thinking, you know the mental aspect of our lives is very important to me. We cannot be effective if our mind is dull. It hampers our thinking and causes us to make a poor choice which then brings about negative consequences in our daily living. You can improve this area by becoming a Bookhead like me. Reading expands and strengthens our mind. Read more on topics you enjoy and expand your reading to new topics. You may also want to take a class at a local university or community college to sharpen your mind.

Then the fourth area is the Spiritual. One can improve in this realm of our being by following their religious heritage. As I have mentioned mine is the Christian heritage. For those without a religious heritage, who may consider themselves agnostic or atheist the spiritual can still have a place in taking time for Mindfulness Meditation, or taking time alone to reflect in nature. Those who follow a religious path need to place into their time schedule a daily time for spiritual development based on their particular teachings. I try each day to find time for devotion and prayer.

How is your saw doing? To live the best life possible we need to take control of our time and place in our schedules time for Sharpening the Saw. As we improve physically, socially, mentally, and spiritually we will have more energy and be more alert for the other major areas in our busy schedule. If we don't it will be like sawing a tree with a dull rusty blade. We won't get the job done and we may even break.

One day before one Christmas I was baking Snicker doodles_and listening to a Bruce Cockburn_Christmas CD, I reminisced over my times of baking Christmas cookies for friends in the past years back when I was in Chicago. I also turned my mind to the importance of savoring memories and savoring in general. Years ago I read the book *Savoring: A New Model of Positive Experience*, by Fred B. Bryant and Joseph Veroff. Their book looks at their 20 years of research on the subject of savoring and its benefits for daily life and enjoyment of life.

Their basic definition of savoring is that people have the "capacities to attend to, appreciate and enhance the positive experiences in their lives." Looking at Merriam Webster's definition of Savor "*it is to season, to taste, to relish or delight in, to enjoy.*" This is such a great term in considering living a more than ok existence. In savoring life we are enjoying and delighting in tasting the moments of our life journey. Savoring is similar to mindfulness in being aware of the present moment but more broad as it encompassed reflections over the past and enjoyment of present activities. It is also similar to Dr. Czikszentmihalyi's concept of flow in that savoring has a timelessness quality to it in that you slow down and just enjoy the sunset or watch the birds at the bird feeder while you are enjoying your morning cup of coffee without thinking about what should come next in your time schedule. Savoring of memories or situations can be done individually or you can have a savoring time with close friends or family.

Of course the stress and hurry of life keeps us looking at the clock instead of the sunset. With the hustle and bustle of the Christmas holiday season I am glad while baking I thought of savoring. Even though the baking for 5 hours was a lot of work in mixing ingredients spooning out cookie dough, with the Christmas music in the background and the smell of finished cookies, I could think back of memories of years ago. Even back to when as a boy I looked forward to a neighbor who would drop by her freshly baked cookies to our home. During one grocery trip during the Christmas season, someone at the grocery store I met talked about how busy she was and since cookie tins are so cheap and time is so lacking buying Christmas cookies is the best way to go. If that gives her more time to savor the Christmas season with her friends and family great but that afternoon of baking helped me think through memories of past Christmas times and gave some fresh baked gifts to give to dear friends.

The benefits of taking time for moments of savoring has been shown to lower stress as you are slowing down for times of reflection on the present experience—such as the awesomeness of enjoying God's creation or even savoring the taste of a delicious home made brownie. Both are savoring moments. The positive feelings that occur through savoring helps build positive emotions and increases happiness levels. Having a savoring mindset also helps us enjoy the journey of life. Too often we are busy getting to the destination which is important; but when I am driving for example I like to point out beautiful gardens or check out the cows grazing in the fields along the way, instead of just staring at the road ahead. Savoring helps us enjoy the journey.

Drs. Bryant and Veroff in their book have an exercise which can help in building a savoring mindset. They encourage for a week to try out a daily vacation of 20 minutes a day. Do something you enjoy—a walk on the beach, reading a favorite book, drinking coffee while listening to music. Try a few different activities during the week not the same thing each day. During this time make a commitment to enjoy yourself—make sure to say no to interruptions. Be totally free and just focus on what you are doing on your daily vacation. As you do your vacation activity take note of feelings you feel and build memories of the experience. Especially take note of positive emotions. After your 20 minute daily vacation experience plan the next vacation experience for the next day. Take a few moments to savor the vacation and reflect over the positive feelings from the previous days vacations. This can be done verbally or in a journal. At the end of the week reflect over and savor each of the daily vacations. Think over the positive feelings you experienced each day. Compare how you feel now over how you feel on a normal week of your life.

Another creative exercise to build up savoring skills in your life is their Camera Exercise. On a sunny day take your camera to a secluded area like a park, beach or a place in the country. Then find an object that catches your attention. It could be a flower, a tree, a building, the waves crashing onto the beach. Now start taking pictures at various angles. Get into a flowing mindset of shooting various pictures of the object. Don't think and judge, just look at alternative shots to take with your camera. Feel the shots that you enjoy taking and don't worry about balance. Try to take 30-40 pictures this way. Finally, as I assume in this digital age and you are using a digital camera; download the pictures to your computer and savor the experience, take time to reflect over the pictures. Ponder how you feel about the pictures and the object you were shooting. If you journal you may want to right down some memories of this experience.

Savoring our journey in this life can help us appreciate the goodness of God in our daily life. We can be more observant of the details that make up our day. Slowing down to notice the roses or another person's smile may help in combating a grumbling attitude. As when we rush through the day, we usually just notice the negative things that irritate us.

Another aspect of Savoring is a deeper appreciation of Nature all around us. I think of a time my wife, daughter and I just had just finished up a vacation traveling from Akron, Ohio to see family and then drove to spend the final days enjoying Niagara Falls, New York. In having a more than ok life it is important to give yourself a break from the daily grind of work. Even if you have a job you love you need the rejuvenation of breaking away for a short time.

When we first arrived in Niagara Falls we took a tour that combined the Cave of the Winds, Maid of the Mist_Boat ride and several other scenic stops. I was skeptical as I felt it was pricey but afterwards we realized it gave us a chance to see numerous facets of the Niagara falls area since we only had a couple of days there. The tour also gave us a wealth of historical information from our tour guide. His name was Prady and called all of us in his van the "Prady Bunch". I could tell he had a passion for what he was doing. He relished in sharing facts about Niagara Falls and added humor at the right time. If you have just a short time in Niagara I highly recommend to take a guided tour.

The next day we went back to Niagara Falls State Park. Walking through the park we were able to enjoy the beauty of the Falls at various angles. The majestic flow of the water and creative beauty of the rainbows at the base of the Falls on a sunny day, made me wonder how people cannot believe there is a Creator God.

That is for me to keep wondering about and will share more on this in a future section on spirituality. I went back and forth from appreciation of the creation of nature around me to viewing the people of diverse nations who were visiting Niagara Falls. From young children to aging seniors, each face I saw had the same look of appreciating the rapturous views of the water falls.

Even though it was a diverse crowd the beauty of enjoying and appreciating nature created a oneness beyond racial barriers. I have noticed people at parks are more open to be friendly. Here at Niagara and I have seen this at other parks; even though some people could not communicate because of language barriers a gesture to take a picture of a couple or family so someone did not have to be left out brought out brighter smiles. So consider on a future vacation to take in a national or state park. Soak in the visual splendors of creation in the trees, water, flowers, animal life. Enjoy meeting new people from diverse cultures who come to visit the parks.

Savoring is deeply soaking in experiences as you are going through them. It is taking time to reflect on the present moment so as to imbed the moment into our memory. When we are savoring, it often also brings up corresponding memories. I remember visiting at Lost Maples State Park in Texas, with my family and taking photos that afternoon allowed me to reflect on memories of Fall trips when I was young in Ohio to the various state parks Ohio is noted for. Those were positive times with my mother, brother and family friends growing up. The Fall colors also brought back memories of the many Fall weekend hikes in the Chicago area. Many a Saturday I would hike from Peterson Avenue on the far North side and follow the lakefront parks to the North Avenue Beach area. Memories of good times bring happiness into your life.

As I remember the trip to Lost Maples we stayed in a cabin. During the late evening I marveled at all the stars sparkling on the clear backdrop of a black cloud free night sky. It had been many years since I had seen so many stars. Then in the early morning I sat out on the cabins patio to read. I would glance up from the book listening to the sound of silence and marveling at the expanse of trees on the other side of the river. I breathed up a prayer of thankfulness to the Designer Creator behind all the beauty around me.

Taking short breaks to savor the wonder and beauty of nature helps to revive us from the humdrum boredom of life. Opportunities like these help to slow down our pace so we can savor new time moments with family and renew older memories that make life more meaningful. Our minds can tell us we are too busy to take a break or we don't have the money. We almost allowed those voices to stop us from going to Lost Maples. After the weekend experience we were glad that we made the choice to go and get away.

Building the Habit of Savoring is important in making the best use of our time. This savoring of life's moments allows up to appreciate the little things God sends along to brighten our days. Holidays can provide time to slow down and savor the memories from the distant past and this past year. Writing Christmas cards to friends bring up memories of past interactions and activities with those who have been close over the years. Christmas school plays and holiday church services bring back memories of childhood to reminisce while sipping hot cinnamon apple cider. Christmas is a natural time to savor life as it is a holiday season that has so many memories attached to it. Since it is at the end of the year it allows as a good point to reflect over the events of the past year.

Living the more than ok life we need to savor life throughout the year not just at the end of the year. The benefits of savoring life each week is that we lower our stress levels as we learn to slow down and smell the roses in our daily life. Much of our stress and anxiety come from being on the go, go, go track of life and not noticing what is really going on in our lives. Our lack of in the present mindfulness makes our lives disjointed and disconnected which increases our stressed out feelings of being out of control.

Lisa Graham McMinn author of The Contented Soul: The Art of Savoring Life has this to say about savoring life: "We are surrounded by simple pleasures and the possibility of sipping and savoring our very earthy, very physical life. Contentment awaits us, inviting to savor each moment, and in doing so to honor the God who gave us life". In her book she gives practical exercises to savor the world around us and to savor our relationship to God. Building up the habit of savoring helps us to see the importance of slowing our lives down, so we can enjoy life and living more.

With savoring, instead of scattering our thoughts continually we learn to take a deep breath and focus on the hummingbird at the feeder; the colored leaves on the tree in autumn; watching the variety of people walking through the mall, while we sit enjoying a cup of coffee. It is appreciating creation and the little joys of life which leads to being thankful in our spirits to the Creator God. Savoring is a habit that brings joy and relaxation into our lives.

Another benefit to savoring it yields the fruit of contentment in our lives which counters the constant urge for more and more stuff in our lives. I think of how Christmas has been turned into a consumer buy-a-thon instead of celebrating God's loves and grace to mankind in the story of Jesus. We can live richer lives in savoring and appreciating what we have instead of a continual angst to desire more and more of the newest technology to hit the market.

One passage from the writings of the Apostle Paul in Philippians 4:8 relates to this, "And now, dear brothers and sisters, let me say one more thing as I close this letter. Fix your thoughts on what is true and honorable and right. Think about things that are pure and lovely and admirable. Think about things that are excellent and worthy of praise . . . . For I have learned how to get along happily whether I have much or little. I know how to live on almost nothing or with everything. I have learned the secret of living in every situation, whether it is with a full stomach or empty, with plenty or little." Be content and savor, soak in all the good in life. If our minds, our thinking, are focused on the good in life and all that is lovely around us we are savoring. We are taking the time to slow down and truly enjoy the life God wants us to enjoy.

When time manages us we are always rushed and stressed and can miss out on beauty that is happening around us. Here is an example of that. It comes from a Sunday church message the Preaching Elder told a story that relates to our changing how we use our time. To learn to slow down in life to capture the moments of beauty and joy that God places in our paths but we are too hurried to notice them. The story was a true one of a study done by the Washington Post to see how people use their time and their priorities. Do people recognize real talent in unlikely places? They had Joshua Bell, a famous violinist, go to a Washington D.C. transit station. In the lobby he played for about 45 minutes. How many people of the crowd of hundreds of passerbys would stop, listen and enjoy the talented musician?

The study found that only a handful of the hundreds that passed through actually stopped to enjoy his violin music. If only they knew people pay hundreds of dollars to hear Joshua Bell play in concert halls. The video reminded me of my time of living in Chicago taking the trains for transportation. Many times at the station there would be street musicians playing. Most of the time, depending how busy I was; I would take a few minutes to listen and if I really enjoyed the music I would toss some coins or a dollar in their case or box. Why? Because, I enjoyed the beauty of the music. The sharing of their talent many times made my day better. Far too many people are too busy to take the time to enjoy a little portion of beauty that God drops into their lives.

Some may say catching a train is very important so they were right to rush by the musician. Yes, I did have my rushed days where running to the train was the most important issue. The important issue the Washington Times experiment drives home still, is do we stay in the rushed mode all the time or take times to savor the little beauties in life that come our way. Do we have to always quickly rush into the garage and miss the hummingbird in the front yard flower garden?

Jesus in the gospel writings says "Consider the lilies of the field, how they grow; they neither toil nor spin, yet I tell you, even

Solomon in all his glory was not arrayed like one of these." (Matt. 6:28-29). In the context the meaning is focusing on overcoming our anxiety and worry. Yet in relation to being mindfully aware and savoring the beauty in life which the Joshua Bell story speaks to; we need to consider, take notice of the beauty of the lily to learn what Jesus is getting at. If we are too rushed and hurried in life to notice the lilies that come into our lives we can't learn from the beauty around us.

In making the most of our life take time to take note of the little things in each day of your life journey. Learn to slow down. Go to www.slowmovement.com for ideas. The little beauties and joys can perk up a dull boring day or brighten a downright terrible day. At the same time do not forget the big joys as well. One stressful week at work ended and my wife and I enjoyed a treat as jazz great Ramsey Lewis performed a concert at our local Arts Center. The concert was 90 minutes of sheer joy with an ending with inspiration as he ended his concert with a medley of gospel songs, Precious Lord and Amazing Grace. Looking for Joy and Beauty in each day helps you in living a more than OK life!

Another way of appreciating nature and savoring nature came to me as I stumbled upon a group that focuses in on Appreciating Clouds. At a conference I was attending, during one of my sessions an attendee mentioned there was a Cloud Appreciation Society. At first mention I thought it strange to have an organization about clouds. Upon returning home I looked up their website— cloudappreciationsociety.org. I marveled at their photo gallery of cloud pictures.

The next few days I caught myself looking up into the sky admiring the cloud formations around me. This brought back memories of younger days staring at the clouds and seeing shapes in the clouds. I don't know if you ever did such things when you were young. It was amazing what you could dream up looking at the clouds. It was very relaxing and I realized it still is.

I have a beautiful view of the sky and clouds from my home office desk. This is very inspirational spot to look outside and appreciate nature. Sometimes there is a squirrel perched on the fence munching on some seeds. But since hearing about the Cloud Appreciation Society, it is the sky and clouds that often catch my attention. Looking at the clouds is peaceful and allows my mind to slowdown. Savoring life and learning to slowdown and to appreciate the simple things in life is part of living more than ok.

The vastness of the sky dotted with puffy clouds makes me think of the Grand Creator behind the beauty of creation. Taking five or ten minutes to relax and savor the Cloudscapes helps me to calm down so I can focus anew on the activities I am trying to accomplish. We need to work and accomplish our tasks but we also need to rejuvenate by savoring God's Creation.

Here is one thought from the Cloud Appreciation Society's Manifesto:

> "Clouds are so commonplace that their beauty is often overlooked. They are for dreamers and their contemplation benefits the soul. Indeed, all who consider the shapes they see in them will save on psychoanalysis bills."

One point that stands out to me in the statement is how the beauty of clouds are overlooked. That is often true of so many things in our lives. How in our over hurried lives we miss the small beauties around us that can improve our daily outlook. We need to look to the sky and dream new dreams from the inspiration we see.

Another way to improve our use of time is to consider the question how would life be different you us if we knew we only had a month to live? That is an important question to consider in Living More Than OK. Sometime ago a dear friend gave my wife and I the book One Month To Live by Kerry & Chris Shook. The Shook's are the founders of the Fellowship of the Woodlands in the suburbs of Houston, Texas. A little over 10 years have passed since I had my brush with death, but stent surgery to my heart arteries saved my life. So thinking of this anniversary made me think about this book.

The premise of the book, looking at our life journey with the end in mind, is very relevant to how I have lived my life since the stents unblocked my two blocked heart arteries. Knowing that ten years ago may have been my last day has affected how I lived since then and today. The experience gave me renewed purpose for living life and that God had a purpose for my life continuing. That purpose is still cloudy sometimes yet each new morning I awake I know there is a reason to use my time wisely.

The authors early on in the book bring up an interesting analogy by mentioning cemetery grave markers. Every time I visit my hometown of Barberton, Ohio I try to visit my parent's gravesite. The markers list their birthdate then a dash and then the day they passed away from this life. The authors note that we don't choose our birth date and the day we die but the dash, which is the time in between we can make choices on how we use it. How very true. Do we consider how to maximize the use of our dash time?

We can live a better life if we take seriously to make the most of our dash time. One could think of the book title and think this is a morose way to live. Waking up and hiding under the covers as, "This might be the day I die. I think I will stay inside and watch Reality TV re-runs." That is not the message of the book. When we accept our mortality we are more open to living life in a way that we can make the most of it, and hopefully impact it in a way to improve the lives of others.

In Ecclesiastes 7:4 it reads, "A wise person thinks much about death, while the fool only thinks about having a good time now." By accepting our mortality we can make better choices with how we want to use our dash time to make the most of the fleeting time in this life. By just living for pleasurable impulses we may miss some really great opportunities that we may have enjoyed even more. The fool is just reacting to life and not thinking through how he or she wants to really live their life.

The authors speak to important topics that are found in making a flourishing life. Having a strong connected spiritual relationship to God is the foundation of life so this is highlighted in the book as primary. This relationship should be of main importance in our dash time. Relationships with others are also stressed by the authors. Too many people die and those left behind have unresolved issues because relationships were not a priority. To live a life without regrets it is important to work on relationship issues in the land of the living.

Living passionately and being open to risk taking are important and so are discussed by the authors. Many come to the end of their lives with regrets because they did not do what they wanted to do in life. They always had certain things on their "get around to it" list but they never really got to them. That is one problem with such lists. We make the lists but allow the mundane activities of life to snuff out the importance of the items we really want to do.

Psalm 37:4 says "Delight yourself in the Lord and He will give you the desires of your heart." If your primary connection to God is right and He has placed a passion in your heart for something then take the risk to do it instead of putting it on a "get around to it" list that will be quickly covered up the others cares and day to day business of life. The importance thing about this verse of scripture is the first part. Too many people claim this as a promise for going after our desires. The text clearly shows the priority is having a right relationship to God and then the desires, passionate items, can be gone after with knowing God will be with us.

An important feature of the book I found is the "Make It Last For Life" reflection boxes at the end of each chapter. The questions help to savor the information so you can apply it to your everyday life. It is sort of a paradox being faced in this book. To truly live life to its fullest, we need to consider our death and what kind of legacy we wish to leave behind.

Reading the Shook's book reminded me the importance of numbering our days. That phrase popped into my mind after hearing a church message about numbering our days. We need personal reflection times to look at the long range decades of our lives and the numbering of our days. There are two Biblical references to the concept of numbering our days.

Psalm 39:4 "Show me, O LORD, my life's end and the number of my days; let me know how fleeting is my life." The emphasis of the Psalm is the reality of how brief our life is. In verse 5 David goes on to say, "Each man's life is but a breath." No matter how long you can hold your breath; a breath is not a long time. David seems to be complaining to God in the text. Commentators on the passage, bring to light that he may be reflecting over the many difficulties in his life; such as his years of being on the run from King Saul even though David was anointed as King. He had to have been heartbroken by also being chased away by his own son, Absalom at one point in time. He had many tragedies and sad hurtful emotions that he took before God. Looking again at the text in verses 2 & 3, "my anguish increased. My heart grew hot within me". Here are feelings of anger and anxiety King David is experiencing. These feelings are not wrong instead, it is what we do with them. Here he is bringing them to God in prayer. If he lived today he would have been tempted to star in a reality TV show and rage against the injustices in his life. But something tells me being the man after God's own heart he still would have taken the feelings to God in his quiet time and would reject TV deals. In difficult times and times of regret we often realize how short a time our life journey is. This Psalm is a reminder don't wait for difficulties to come to take time to reflect on numbering our days.

The other Psalm that has the phrase is Psalm 90:12, "Teach us to number our days aright, that we may gain a heart of wisdom." The overall context of this Psalm exalts God's greatness in His eternal nature versus the brevity of our lives. In this Psalm, David is not looking in anguish at the end of his life. Instead he is seeking God's wisdom in how to make his life count for God. He wants to understand the time he has left so that he can use it wisely. Wisely for the work God has for him. This is seen in the final verse 17, "May the favor of the Lord our God rest upon us; establish the work of our hands for us—yes, establish the work of our hands." He repeats the phrase "establish the work of our hands", so the Psalmist David sees this as an important element of using our time, "our days", in a wise manner.

Charles Spurgeon in his Treasury of David has this to say about this verse, *"A short life should be wisely spent. We have not enough time at our disposal to justify us in misspending a single quarter of an hour. Neither are we sure of enough of life to justify us in procrastinating for a moment. If we were wise in heart we should see this, but mere head wisdom will not guide us aright."* Spurgeon is right. If we look at the emphasis in both passages we see the brevity of life. If our life goes by so quickly and time is one way to honor God, we need to be wise in using the gift of time. At the end of Psalm 90 David is seeking God's favor, His blessing, for God to establish His work in David. I don't believe this is speaking only our vocational work even though it is important. In our numbering our days we need to look at all the variety of works God has for us to do and then use our time wisely to honor God in these works.

The idea of numbering our days reminds me of Stephen Covey's principle of "Begin with the end in mind" As we look into the next year, 5 years or next decade to see where we want to go and accomplish we are visualizing a mind picture or a blue print of what the end results look like. Covey states, "If you don't make a conscious effort to visualize who you are and what you want in life, then you empower other people and circumstances to shape you and your life by default. It's about connecting again with your own uniqueness and then defining the personal, moral, and ethical guidelines within which you can most happily express and fulfill yourself." These thoughts line up well with King David's in Psalm 90 to seek a heart of wisdom to see the work ahead that God has for us.

To end this section before considering a related song is to consider taking a break from technology to enjoy use of our time. Another way to take a break away for the hectic life we lead and to enjoy a Living More Than OK Life it helps to take a break from technology.

Technology is so much of our daily lives and we often we can not do without it. Much of our work involves the computer screen many hours a day. Emails and texts seem to be never ending. Even in grocery stores in produce sections I see people picking up vegetables or fruits with one hand and scrolling their iphone screens with the other. I want to walk up them and say "why don't you give it a rest". As a family we gave technology a rest one weekend.

We took a weekend trip to Bastrop State Park, which is outside of Austin, Texas. Instead of doing a hotel with free internet and cable tv, we rented a full service cabin inside the park grounds. The cabins were very simple but comfortable. I was surprised to read of the history of the cabins on a poster inside the cabin. It turned out that they were built in the 1930's by the Civilian Conservation Corps during the Great Depression. I remembered that 3 of my uncles served in the CCC before World War II.

We enjoyed canoeing on the lake and hiking through the woods. Even though there had been a recent fire that devastated the area, we viewed nature making a come back. Many of the pines near the cabins were coming back strong. Further from the lake and into the deeper wooded areas the trees were still more barren. The morning canoe outing was the highlight for my wife and I. It was so relaxing to be out on a still lake viewing the surrounding nature from that perspective. We took the sights in with all our senses to savor the time together and capturing pictures of the beauty of the park. That is one of the positives of taking time to be out in nature to savor God's Creation.

In the evening at the cabin we continued to keep away from technology. There was no television in the cabin. So we spent time playing a game called WhatchamaDRAWit. We had never played it since buying it and had lost the instructions so we made up our own rules and enjoyed playing our version of it. That opened up conversation time which is also a rare item in today's technology world of texting or talking in short phrases. Twitter and Facebook communication has limited communication to just short phrases. It seems like people can't even read an email that asks three topics as they will just respond to whatever the person first stated and ignore the other items in an email. So it was pleasant to be away from the technology to use old fashioned speaking in communication.

The time at the park was so pleasant. We realized the need to break away from technology from time to time. To enjoy life to the fullest it helps to do other things than to be tied to the electronic gadgetry that tries to control our lives. Think of ways you can take a break from technology from time to time.

In closing off this chapter on time I want to look at another song that is one of my favorites, as an example the effect music and lyrics can have for our benefit. The song is Miracle of the Moment, by Steven Curtis Chapman. As with the other songs I have mentioned take time to find it on the internet to do a more in-depth reflection personally about the song. I hope this chapter has given you another look at how to use your time. Traditional time management is important so we use our time wisely. Then we will have time in our lives to savor and enjoy more of the moments.

This song speaks to an important part of *Living More Than OK*, in relation to time. Making the most of each moment, by appreciating each moment can have a dynamic effect in our lives. We can increase our happiness levels in life if we can appreciate each moment in our time line as a miracle. By buzzing around busily, we miss the wonder of the world around us. That is a key element I see Chapman is getting across to us in his song.

I know too many times I have missed the sunsets, and here in Texas, we have some beautiful ones. I have passed by the flowers unknowingly of their beauty. I have missed the treasures of relating to the people around me—to enjoy sharing their joys or helping with their hurts. Why? I am too caught up rushing on a train to nowhere or blindly floating on autopilot routinely doing tasks that have no lasting value. Do you ever find yourself this way? Be active in your present with awareness as our choices in the present have a great impact on our futures. As Chapman writes, "And this is the only moment we can do anything about".

Reflections for chapter 6: *Here are a variety of reflections in relation to savoring and making the most of your time.*

Rate yourself in the four areas: Physical, Social, Mental, and Spiritual. Which area are your strongest in? Which area do you need the most growth in?

What physical activities are you involved in?

How are you working to improve your most significant relationships?

How are you improving your Mental side of your life? Are you reading a new book? Have you considered taking a Continuing Education course at a local College or an online course?

Do you take time each day to improve your spiritual life?

"The aim of life is appreciation." G.K.Chesterton (1936) Make a list of 10 things you are appreciative of in your life. Take time to savor over the list as to memories of why these are important to you. How can you be more appreciative in your daily life? Can you slow down your life and enjoy the journey more?

Spend 10 minutes sitting outside still in a chair. Sit upright and close your eyes. Listen to the sounds around you. Then open your eyes and stay seated and soak in through your eyes all the details of what you see. Write down your feelings of the experience.

Take a walk quietly through your neighborhood or a nature setting without an I-Pod in your ears. Savor the sights, smells and sounds around you during the walk. Write down the feelings of the experience. Go to http://slowdownnow.org and jot down a couple of ideas you can incorporate in your life to help you live more slowly.

Take five to ten minutes to relax and look to the sky and observe the clouds. Jot down in a journal how the clouds make you feel. Write down a few memories of what looking at clouds was like when you were a young child. Also visit the Cloud Appreciation Society website http://cloudappreciationsociety.org and be inspired by their photo gallery. If you are a photographer take some photos of clouds you see.

What would change in your life if you knew you had a month to live? Is there something God has placed a passion in your life for?

Take a day and shut down the electronic technology that you think is vital to your existence. You will see you can survive a day without Facebook or texting. You may even enjoy it. Go to a State park, zoo, museum, or a picnic at a local park. Enjoy a conversation with someone with the cell phone off or silent. Write in a journal how your experience away from technology felt.

Resources for further learning:

Bryant, Fred & Veroff, Joseph, Savoring: A New Model of Positive Experience, Lawrence Erlbaum Associates, 2007

Steven Curtis Chapman, "Miracle of the Moment" This Moment CD 2007.

Covey, Stephen, The 7 Habits of Highly Effective People, Free Press, 1989.

Maxwell, John, Today Matters, Warner Books, 2004

McMinn, Lisa, The Contented Soul, Intervarsity Press, 2006

Shook, Kerry & Chris, One Month To Live, waterbrook Press, 2012

Be Open To Happenstance

It would be nice if we woke up everyday and we knew in advance what would happen each day. Yet we know that is not what life is like. Even for the most organized person who lives and breathes each moment coordinated by their daily planners, happenstance events invade our life. John Krumboltz and Al Levin in their book, *Luck Is NO Accident*, say this about life, "Have you ever noticed that unplanned events—chance occurrences— more often determine your life and career choices than all the careful planning do? A chance meeting, a broken appointment, a spontaneous vacation trip, a "fill-in" job, a newly discovered hobby—these are the kinds of experiences—happenstances—that lead to unexpected life directions and career choices."(page 5). Their book goes on to show story after real story of how happenstance events affected peoples career choices. This chapter will look at this part of life.

Part of happenstance are those times where we catch ourselves saying, "My what a coincidence we meet as I was just thinking of you yesterday." Or you take a new direction in your life and after the fact you remember you chose the direction based on a detail that occurred outside of your control. We think of those events as coincidence or happenstance. What a coincidence. One evening I heard on the Mike Huckabee show an interview with a man named Squire Rushnell. My mind perked up when he started talking about his new book *Divine Alignments and God Winks*—a new way to look at coincidences in our lives.

After hearing him I saw in a bookstore a book he mentioned and other books he had written. The one that caught my attention was

When God Winks. I picked it up and it is a short book so it did not take long to read. The information reminded me of the Drs. Krumboltz & Levin's book *Luck Is No Accident*, which considers our choices in response to happenstances that come into our life experiences. We all have coincidences that pop into our life and the key is how we respond.

At the beginning of Squire's book he lists definitions of key terms. Coincidence "is a sequence of events that although accidental seems to have been planned or arranged", from the American Heritage Dictionary. A Wink "is to give a signal or express a message". He took that definition from the American Heritage Dictionary as well. He then created the term God Wink stating that it is a "personal signal or message, directly from a higher power, usually, but not always, in the form of a coincidence". In the book the author poses a sensible question in that if the term coincidence has a sense of the event being planned or arranged then who does the planning? He states that most people respond that God does the arranging. It is not a proof that there is a God but it makes sense that considering the probabilities of some of the things that happen to us there is some sort of a God guiding our life events.

The book looks at a variety of examples of God Winks in various life situations. Squire Rushnell also shows how we can react to the God Winks. We should not just float along the river of life letting life happenstance events affect us. Life is not to be lived passively as that turns us into victims of fate. Instead with the coincidences or as Mr. Rushnell calls them God Winks, we make a choice to respond actively to these life events. After the choice is made we receive the consequence of our response. That consequence can be either good or bad based on whether we critically thought through our response or just impulsively responded.

The author gives us a series of questions to explore and discover the God Winks that are in our lives. Here are just a few of the questions listed to help you start exploring your God Winks:

Did something surprising happen to you in your past?

Did some new person come into your life?

Did you experience a death of someone close to you? Did this open up a new path for you?

What is the biggest break you have ever received in your career journey?

Did you have a rebirth in a spiritual manner or in another manner such as giving up drugs or alcohol?

His reminder to think through questions reminded me of Dr. Tal Ben Shahar's lectures on Positive Psychology where Dr. Shahar mentioned our questions we ask ourselves can help us create new realities for our daily lives. Those questions can help in exploring the various God Winks that have affected us and then we can look deeper into them and think through the choices we made in response. In exploring God Winks in my life the most of them that I have clearly noticed have often been in church worship times where the minister is preaching and I have this feeling like, "how did he know that about me? That is just what I needed to hear." I am not paranoid at those times, instead thinking about it, the feeling points out that the Pastor's message may be a God Wink reminding me of what I need to work on from the message. Another God wink that comes to mind is my career positions that have focused on helping students in their career focus relates to a Professor at UTB in Brownsville. I had professor for Career Counseling who encouraged us students to be involved in Professional Associations. So I became involved with the National Career Development Association as a student and with the state association CDA in Texas. I would not have joined that association if I had not had that Professor. I believe this also helped me see the importance of careers in people's lives. Was it just chance I had a Professor that encouraged such activities? I do not think so.

Considering God Winks is a helpful reflective exercise to help us be more aware of what is going on in our lives. The more we see God work in our lives the more our lives can make sense out of happenstance items that drop into our life journey. This awareness can help us in understanding out purpose in a deeper fashion as well. You may want to look further into the author's ideas by looking at his facts page of his website—http://www. whengodwinks.com/faqs/ or better yet purchase his books or read them from your local library. With the reflection over happenstance events in our daily lives, it is also important to look at our reaction to the events. That is where Krumboltz & Levin's thoughts align with Squire Rushnell. They title their book Luck Is No Accident because there is always the human response to the "Luck" or "Godwink". The lucky break does not occur if we are not open to the possibility of it and take a chance to grasp a hold of it. That is one key point both books are trying to get across.

Continuing on the thought of happenstance in our life journey map I am reminded of a Keiko Matsui concert we attended as a family. She is one of my favorite musicians. Keiko was showcasing her new CD, *The Road* . . . as well as playing some songs from previous recordings. We were looking forward to the concert as it has been over 10 years since my wife and I had heard her live in Chicago. She was energetic as always and exuded positive energy in her performing. Her new songs showed her continual growth in creativity. There were new styles mixed in with the familiar styles of her older work. That is what lifelong learning is all about— continual growth and stretching to create the new.

The concert was refreshing. Even though I had been sick that week the time in her concert strengthened my body and mind as I mindfully enjoyed listening to her music. She has a knack for having a great band to work with. Each of the players enjoyed what they were playing and are talented musicians each in their own right. I always enjoy a keyboard player who becomes absorbed into their instrument as I can tell the artist is experiencing flow and bringing out the best performance as possible. Keiko is like this and it makes watching and listening to her artistry captivating.

In one of the few times she spoke during the concert she touched on a concept that I want to share with you to ponder and savor in your thinking. She shared that in compiling the CD she was doing personal reflection on her life journey—something I encourage often in my weekly blog. She said she titled the CD, *The Road . . .* as each of our lives are like a road. Each one of us have a uniquely different road to travel with varying twists and turns. Our roads are made up of our relationships, environments, cultures, belief systems. The most important point she stated was that the true title of the CD focuses on the "Dot, Dot, Dot" as she emphasized the three consecutive periods after the word "Road". These simple dots stand for the simple reality that each day of our life our personal Road keeps going on. As with Dr. Krumboltz's Happenstance theory, we do not know for sure what is around the bend or over the hill in our Road. But still we travel on. We travel on with positive anticipation for good ahead. Personally for me that is where my faith in God is often the strongest in knowing that He knows what is around each bend. Her sharing her heartfelt thoughts behind the CD helped me in my own personal reflection during the concert and allowed me to enjoy the experience of the concert on a deeper level. If you ever have the opportunity to hear Keiko Matsui in concert definitely take that opportunity on your road trip through life.

Exploring Possibilities is part of the process of being open to Happenstance. Art always amazes me with the impact it has to affect the emotions and our inner spirit. That is one reason I enjoy viewing art in museums and art shows. I appreciate the artist's talent but also seek to find a message for myself in the artwork. I have an art piece by Kelly Rae Roberts that relates to possibilities. I like to know the stories of artists so I went to her website, http:// kellyraeroberts.com. I was surprised initially to see she studied social work not art in her educational pursuits. She worked as a social worker and when she was 30 she followed her passion into art. She describes herself as a "lover of life and people", on her website. As I think over the pictures I saw in the store of her work that is very true of her artwork. I can see how social worker creatively fits into what she paints.

Her style comes across to me as modern and abstract. But it is not a harsh abstract and to me has a clear message. Her choices of colors feel very calming and positive. Her love of people orientation to me is seen in many of the paintings as she has people in them or positive phrases that can encourage and uplift the human soul.

That is what drew me to the painting I purchased, "Believe in Possibility". There is a path or a road across the middle of the picture which I view it as an ongoing field on the other side with the sky bright with light. The green around the edges add a peaceful feeling to me. The "believe in possibility", stands out in the light of the sky.

Sometimes life is like that, settled on one side of the road, a little dark but comfortable as that is where we are and what we are familiar with. But a dream or a passion we may have, may mean to take a risk across the darker road and follow our field of dreams. We can be stopped from following into the light by saying to ourselves "it is not possible". But two verses come to mind that I thought of in the store when I bought this painting. One is Matthew 19:26 "With people this is impossible, but with God *all things are possible."* *Then in Mark 9:23 "All things are possible* to him who believes." One writer, Matthew focuses in on God in the equation that God makes all things possible and then Mark is looking at our human responsibility to have faith and believe in the God of possibilities.

As I look over my life I have been stopped many times from my lack of faith in possibilities coming true. So I stayed stunted in the foreground of the painting and not enjoying the light on the other side of the path. It is easier too often to say that is impossible to a new opportunity, rather than take a chance to try. This painting now in my office is a reminder that there are future possibilities ahead for the good that I have not even imagined yet. And some even right in front of me that I need to step across the road to enjoy them. I just need to keep faith in the God of possibilities as I step out and cross the road.

Each of us have rainy days of difficulties that come into our lives from time to time. These are unplanned happenstance events that bring trouble to varying degrees. Sometimes the rain feels like a storm pounding you and knocking you around. These events may be a car accident, or an illnesses that hits you out of the blue. Really bad events may seem like a hurricane. The hurricane events may be a sudden death of a loved one, sudden loss of a job, or finding out of an infidelity in a relationship. Other rainy day events may be a dreary cold drizzle which are just the dull boring drudgeries of life that drag you down to that just getting by, just ok feeling.

Just like with the natural weather we can count on rainy days occurring. Life problems come with much less predictability than the rain shower that are predicted in the weather reports. During the rainy days it is hard to process what can be learned through the troubles that come to us. We are usually stuck in Why me mode. As with the real weather rainy days we know the sun will come out eventually. But during an extended time of personal troubles that feel like a stretch of rainy days, we often feel like the sun will never come again. Yet it does the sun will come back into our life.

Christ in His teachings recorded in Mathew 5:45 speaks to this issue, ". . . For He gives His sunlight to both the evil and the good, and He sends rain on the just and on the unjust, too." The "He" in this verse is speaking of God. That all people whoever they are experience sunny days of good times and problems and troubles on the rainy days. Of course we desire to enjoy more good days than bad days. The reality of life is that it comes with good and bad.

Recently I saw on PBS a Jimmy Cliff concert of him at Austin City Limits. At the end of the concert he did his popular song, "I Can See Clearly Now". It made me think of rainy times in my life and yes the Sun does come back. Here are the lyrics of the song's chorus

> "I can see clearly now the rain is gone I can see all obstacles in my way
>
> Here's the rainbow I've been praying for It's gonna be a bright, bright sunshinin' day
>
> It's gonna be a bright, bright sunshinin'"

When we lived in South Texas where we have a lot of sun compared to when I was living in Chicago. Sometimes we have so much sun people long for rain. Down there after the rain of a hurricane or a long stretch of cloudy rainy days during Winters rainy season it feels so great to see the sun again. It is like the sun is appreciated more after a rainy day. How I remember the cold dreary Winters in Chicago wishing for the sun. Peoples spirits always lightened when the sun would break up the dreariness of Winter cloudy skies. The same is true of the problems that feel like rainy days. Once the sunshine of days finally going right or solutions to problems occur or happenstance surreptitiously brings good our way we feel so much better than ok. As the song sings "we can see clearly now". After the rain we find new directions in our life the sky of our life journey is more of a bright blue. We can handle the obstacles of life with more confidence. We can refocus on the true North of our purpose God has for us in our journey.

Next time the rains come. Remember that you're not alone. We all experience the rain. God is watching over us in the rain. Then you can be confident the rainbow and the sun will return.

Thinking back to another point I picked up from Dr.Krumboltz is that we need to be aware of what is happening in our lives. How often do we notice what is going on around us in the world and people's lives? At the end of one year I read a fiction book, The Noticer, by Andy Andrews. My wife heard Andy speak at a Women Of Faith conference. Andy Andrews has a gift of being a great story teller. In the start of this book the reader is quickly caught up in the story so it is a book that is hard to put down.

The book's key figure, Jones, keenly shows up in a person's life during a time of difficulty. While reading, I debated in my mind whether Jones is a figure of a Guardian Angel or Jesus as he often appears out of nowhere and disappears afterwards. Also the various ethnicities in the book perceive Jones as being of their ethnicity. The importance of the book in my viewpoint is Jones' improving the moral character of the people he is in contact with.

A driving point of the book is that of our attitude in relating to problems that face us. Jones also emphasizes our attitudes are shaped by our perception. A common example of the power of perception is the glass half full or half empty? Our choices we make are being guided by our attitudes and perceptions. Our perceptions in our daily journey can lead to a negative cast down spirit or to a positive spiraling up outlook on life.

Jones is the "Noticer" in the book as he is a watcher of people and notices when they need help. This is a thread in the book that caught my attention as I look at life. The concept relates well with living life mindfully aware. If I am a Noticer, God can use me more through each day in making me notice people He is bringing into my daily journey for the purpose of being His hands and heart to help them. We may seek to serve God by helping others but then become caught up in unaware living so we do not notice the needs that are actually around us. This is where Jones as the Noticer, can help us understand the importance of being aware of how life is playing out around us.

There was something else I relearned in the initial interaction of Jones with another lead character, who was definitely a glass half empty in his perception of life. The importance of learning from historical figures is a lesson Jones teaches the other lead character as a young teenager. In his initial contact with Jones, as homework the teen is handed biographies of Winston Churchill, Will Rogers, George Washington Carver. The young man's perspective of this idea was "boring history books", but Jones' perspective was these were opportunities to look at adventures of great people and learn what made them great.

The young man soon found out that reading these books were interesting and not boring. So Jones gave him other biographies: Joan of Arc, Abraham Lincoln, Victor Frankl, Harry Truman, Florence Nightingale, King David, Harriet Tubman, Queen Elizabeth I, John Adams, Eleanor Roosevelt, Mark twain, Joshua Chamberlain, George Washington, Anne Frank, and Christopher Columbus. In reading these books he saw what Jones was getting at;

that positive values could be learned from the lives of great people as they were people just like him. If they were great he could be great too.

Stories of people's lives can be powerful influencers to learn from to better our own life. As I look at the list Jones recommended there are several I have read and appreciated and learned from. The list also gave me ideas of lives I want to read about in the coming year. Being a Noticer, as seen in this book, means being open, to be an active helper for lives in my sphere of life. Jones did not notice just for people-watching sake. He noticed so he could come along someone struggling in life and help change their perspective so to help them grow to be a better person.

Being open to happenstance comes from our savoring of past memories of events along our road. It is good to take time to reflect on paths we have taken in our lives. Each of us on our journey through life take a variety of pathways in our life journey.

One day my wife sent me an email with a song by trumpeter Chris Botti embedded in it. The song's name was "The Way Home." I enjoyed the song and searched for it on the internet as I wanted to find the cd it was from.

The melody of the song is very catchy and has a feeling of a traveling song. I could imagine myself strolling down a pathway or listening to it in a car stereo traveling down a road home. Then as I was looking at the video that accompanied the song on Youtube, the photography showed a variety of pathways. This caused me to think of pathways to various homesteads in my life. The first one I remembered was my drives from Chicago, from school breaks and holidays to visit Ohio with my mother while she was still living. I usually always took the same pathway of the Indiana and Ohio turnpikes. In the Winter many times the path was slick and icy. In warmer weather when I was young I usually traveled home at night and would drive the turnpike with my windows rolled down with Kansas or Deep Purple blaring from the speakers to keep me awake.

This remembrance reminded me of my visits with mom that I enjoyed and missed after she passed away.

Another pathway that came to mind was when I lived on the far North side of Chicago on Peterson Avenue. I had one favorite pathway especially during a period of time I was going through some difficulties and depression. I would walk from Peterson Avenue on the far North side down to North Avenue Beach. In the Spring and Summer this walk would give me time to reflect on issues in my life and think over ideas for the future. I always enjoyed the people watching as well as the exercise the walk gave me. Getting out of the apartment and enjoying the journey on this Chicago pathway, helped me through some of my most difficult and dark days during that period of time in Chicago.

Then another important pathway I will mention amidst the myriad of pathways I have had in my life is a pathway from Chicago to Brownsville, TX. That was a pathway to where I married my wife in Brownsville, TX. That was a move of uncertainty leaving friends in Chicago and a great city environment. That was a pathway that initially had much uncertainty. I must say the move was one of the best decisions I have made. From that point on my pathways for the future are in unison with my wife. Of course one thing I pick up from the energy in Chris Botti's song The Way Home, is that each path way has its own positive energy and beauty so I have a hope that the future years new pathways will be just as beautiful.

Take some time to reflect over some of the pathways home in your past years of your life journey. What were some of the hills and valleys you faced in the pathway? Every path has pitfalls and holes we trip over. But if we mindfully reflect over our pathways we can be reminded of the beauty in each pathway and reflect over the joy in the journey that we experienced. Many of the aspects of your pathway journeys you will have to admit are filled with happenstance and Godwinks.

We all have times of regret in our life journey. Sometimes the regrets come through difficult happenstance events crashing into our lives. Other times regrets come through foolish choices and foolish actions. In living a more than ok life the aim is to keep regrets to a minimum. I say minimum as try as we like, difficulties that come across as negative, will always appear from time to time in this life.

One way to keep negative regrets to a minimum is to have regular times of reflection in our time schedules to look over how life is going and review choices we are making to see if there is a better way of handling our life journey. Recently I came across a song that speaks to this point. It is by a band named Sister Hazel. A Department Director, where I used to work at told me about the band. Their style is alternative rock with a folk-rock, Southern rock flavor to their sound. Other than enjoying their musical style I appreciated the depth they have to their lyrics. Most of the songs have a positive tone to the message or realistically makes the listener think through an issue.

Think over the lyrics to "Better Way" by Sister Hazel by looking up their video on the internet. Think through what is being said in the context about a life of regrets. How many times do we say in life, "if I could only turn the clock back"; 'this is no way to live"; "There must be a better way of doing this". We are saying these things often after a negative occurrence in our lives. Usually after an event I find myself thinking over it and saying to myself, "What was I thinking I should have done that instead!" If I had a dollar for every time I said that—I would be a billionaire. But as the song said at the beginning time does not bend, we can not turn the clock back and re-say the damaging things we said or re-do the damaging actions we did towards others or even ourselves.

Yet we can change the future by taking time to reflect on present circumstances and think over better ways of making new choices to reshape our next step in life's journey. We can't change the past, but we can ask forgiveness for past mistakes. This allows us to change our futures for the better. Another phrase that stood out to me in the song was "This is no life to live, you gotta give." It made me think of the Biblical thought in Acts 20:35, "In everything I did,

I showed you by this kind of hard work we must help the weak, remembering the words the Lord Jesus himself said, "It is better to give than to receive." A life of taking from others leads to regrets. A secret to a better life is to learn to give of yourself to others. This is so contrary to how we often act but if we reflect on the best times of our lives; it is often when we were not thinking of our self interest but helping others and sharing with others.

An important reminder as we are open to happenstance events and Godwinks if we keep a positive mindset we can answer the following questions with a personal affirmative response. Do I really make a difference in life? Do I really matter? I have heard it said, "Everything you do matters. Every move you make, every action you take . . . matters." With God in the picture we do matter. We are each unique and are created to be difference makers in the world. We may not create a food product that saves billions of lives from famine. But each one of us can make an impact on those around us. That impact only time and history will reveal in the future.

This further reminds me of the importance of our choices and how we live. To be difference makers we need to consciously be aware that our actions can make effects for the positive or the negative in our future and the future of others around us. With each action we make, we then create a reaction in the world. With each decision we make there are consequences that affect our lives which then create new decisions. In this process we can either spiral down in negativity or spiral upwards in a positive direction. I choose to spiral upwards.

Reflections:

Take 30 minutes of quiet time to think through what is going on in your life. Is there a better way to be doing what you are presently doing? Think through are you a Giver or a Taker? What is one way in the next week you could give to others around you more?

Try to remember and write down three God Winks or happenstance events in your life. Ponder over them and write down how these affected your life at the time and events further along your life journey.

What does "Believe in Possibility" mean to you? Is there new possibilities facing you and you need to step out in faith to give them a try?

Try being a Noticer today. See if there is an opportunity to help a family member, friend or even a stranger during your daily journey today. At the end of the day take a few moments to journal thoughts on the experience of helping someone as to how it felt and how did you happened to notice the need to step into the other person's struggle.

Resources for further learning:

Andrews, Andy, The Noticer, Thomas Nelson Publisher, 2011.

Krumboltz, John, & Levin, Al, Luck Is No Accident: Making The Most of Happenstance in Your Life and Career, Impact Publishers, 2004.

Rushnell, Squire, When God Winks, Atria Books, 2001.

Sister Hazel, "Better Way", Chasing Daylight—CD, 2003.

Dream Big and Reach Your Goals

As I stated at near the beginning of this book, sloughing through life in OK mode leads to a life as Henry David Thoreau verbally pictured, "The mass of men lead lives of quiet desperation." A great number of people move through life unfulfilled—watching reality TV, spending free time roaming shopping malls, or surfing the internet or absorbed in their iphones. Not living up to the potential that is within. One of the many ways to Live More Than OK is how I often sign off on emails to students—"Follow Your Dreams!"

Developing your dreams and following them unleashes potential in your life to maximize your experiences. Walt Kallestad says in his book Wake Up Your Dreams, (can be found in libraries or used bookstores), "Dreams can help us see the invisible, believe the incredible, and achieve the impossible." Creating dreams of what you want out of life can wake up passions for new hobbies, life adventures, new career paths, and new relationships. They allow us to achieve more in life than we could ever imagine!

John Maxwell in his recent book, *Put Your Dreams to the Test*, mentions how some people live their lives based on the dreams of others. This is seen in young people doing sports their parents want them to do. Students who aim for careers their parents want them to do. This can cause lack of fulfillment and future anxiety as we were not made to live another's dreams. We were made to live the dreams we were meant to live. Maxwell then takes the reader through a series of questions to reflect over in creating and developing their own dream.

One of the best examples of a person who is an amazing dream maker and dream follower is a man named John Goddard. His story amazed me when I came upon it while internet surfing ideas for a lecture to students on dreams and goal setting. I have used it ever since, with College students to open their minds to the potential each one has to do so many things in their lifetime. John when he was age 15 on a rainy day took out a pad of paper and wrote out 127 things on his "My Life List". The list included places he wanted to go, things he wanted to learn, careers he wanted to follow. Some of his adventures in traveling around the world are noted in his book, *The Survivor.* Here are some examples from his list: explore the Nile river, climb Mt. Ararat, visit every country in the world, visit the Great Wall of China, visit The Taj Mahal, ride an elephant, study native medicines follow the John Muir Trail, high jump 5 feet, read the entire Bible, read the works of Tolstoy, Plato and Aristotle, play Claire De Lune on the piano. At the time of writing his book he had completed 111 of his original list and expanded the list to 500 items. That is what I call dreaming big. What I admire about the story as well is; he did not stick to just his list of 127, but has kept over his years expanding his possibilities. Do check out his website and read his amazing story—http://www.johngoddard.info/index.htm

You may say how does this relate to my previous chapter on our choices towards Happenstance events or as I see them as God Moments, or Godwinks. If happenstance is where it's at, why plan anything or dream dreams?? In life is full of things just happening to us why plan and dream. I have had the privilege of hearing Dr. Krumboltz speak on the issue of Happenstance and life. He points out that he is not against dreaming or goal setting. Instead he encourages people to be open and flexible to new possibilities instead of rigidly hanging on to your dreams. Hanging on to a dream may bring you near destruction. I remember when working at a warehouse when I was younger; I had lunch with a lady who shared how she had been almost killed by her ex-husband and needed plastic surgery from the beatings. I asked her why she stayed so long with him until the near fatal beating. She replied she had thought he was her dream prince charming. A dream that nearly killed her. Again thinking of John Goddard's list, he after many years did not complete everything on his list, instead he opened his mind to many more new possibilities.

I have mentioned songs throughout this book The First song I want to look at speaks of rekindling our dreams. What stops us in following our dreams? Why do our lives get turned upside down and lose sight of the path we were on in our life journey? Why do people of faith have feelings that God has disappeared from involvement in their lives?

Dreams become squelched by the stuff of life overwhelming us. Instead of using wise active choices to control what we can, we passively move about on autopilot and let life situations and dull drudgery control us. Day to day distractions grow and grow until we give up on living more than ok and settle for mundane existence. Then our dreams fade away.

It is sometimes hard to imagine how this can happen. For example, a person who goes off to college with high hopes of a college degree does not plan on not finishing. Yet he may stop out for a year to save up a little more money with the intention to go back soon. Ten years later he never goes back as more and more bills pile up. Another person who wants to start a photography hobby, or learn a musical instrument, she then lets work, housing chores, and other activities take over—never gets around to it. People actually then say "I will get around to it some day". Some day never comes, then regrets take over with all the entailing negativity.

There is a song by one of my favorite musicians, Phil Keaggy's, "Dream Again", comes to my mind as I was thinking over this topic of rekindling dreams. I will give an overview of my thoughts on it but I encourage you to search for it on the internet and listen to the song then reflect over what Phil is saying about dreaming again.

He speaks of feeling upside down and I can relate to his thoughts of feeling upside down when a dream has been lost. When we have lost track of our dreams we do feel out of sorts. As I mentioned at the beginning, it is all the distractions of life that hinder us with our dreams and our wrong reactions lead to giving up on our dreams. We wind up giving up on God and give up on ourselves. I appreciate the picture of him being ready with open hands turned upside down. He is not tensed up clenching wildly on to his distractions. He is ready to move on with dreams for his life and letting go of his distractions so they can fall away. The phrasing reminds me of a single mom, who attended a church in Chicago where I worshipped years ago. Her favorite phrase was "Let go and let God." We can't rekindle lost dreams or create new dreams, if we keep hanging on to life's past difficulties and hurts.

Here is one, *More Than OK*, idea for you to consider and try. In Phil's song he repeats "I will pray". If you are in a period of feeling dreamless and desire to rekindle the fire of personal dreams in your life, get away for a day by yourself. Go to the beach, rent a cabin in the woods, or visit a mountainside retreat. Some place you find relaxing. Make it a spiritual dream retreat day. Pray and meditate over your life. If you are a reader who is not into prayer, simply meditate. Let go of the reactions of the past and distractions of the present. Brainstorm ideas for dreams—new ones and old ones you had forgotten about. In your brainstorming write dream lists out. Write for about 20 minutes on where do you see yourself 5 years from now if you follow some of your dream ideas? Repeat the exercise later expanding the timeline up to 10 years in the future. We are not placed on this earth to live tensely distracted but to live joyfully and abundantly.

I usually pick all my favorite songs but one day a friend knowing some of my blog postings look at songs and their meanings for our life experience sent me the song, *If I Ruled the World*, by Leslie Bricusse_and Cyril Ornadel that was sung by Tony Bennett_back in the 1960's. The song makes me think of the personal power we have in our choices to improve our lives and the lives of those around us. Shad Helmstetter in his book *Choices* states, *"Who knows what you could accomplish in life if you made more of the right choices along the way." Part of following our dreams is making the choice to follow and aim for our dreams.* Each day by the choices we make, we rule our world. The question is what kind of world are we creating? Visualize yourself as ruler of the world and reflect over the words to this song that you can find on the internet.

Why this song makes me think of the power of our choices, is pondering over what I would do if I ruled the world for a day? As we step out each day don't we by our choices make rulings on how our individual worlds will be created and run? There are many positive desires and choices, Leslie Bricusse presents in his lyrics, that are a guide to the kind of choices we can make in Living More Than OK.

In the very beginning he pronounces "ev'ry day would be the first day of spring". Spring is a season of new creation and creativity as flowers and plants bloom. What if we carried that attitude and choice into each day? Looking at each day as a refreshing adventure, instead of a dreary struggle to fight through. No wonder stress and depression is so high when the daily attitude is anticipating the grey storm clouds in the daily journey instead of looking forward to the blooming roses in the day's activities. The phrase, "we'd sing of the joy every morning would bring" reminded me of memories riding the Chicago subway trains in the morning to work. There was never much joy on the faces of people on their way to work. How would the workday change if there was more joy in the attitude choices we make in our day? The song also speaks of smiles as bright as moon beams and happiness. Smiles and a cheery attitude can be a part of how we rule our day for the better in helping to spread joy to the stressed out worker at the cash register, the bus driver, or someone fighting the Monday Morning Blues. Have you ever noticed an attitude in a crabby store worker when you smile and say have a nice day. They immediately for the most part brighten up.

Another standout phrase is "we would treasure each day that occurred". We should rule our world with the attitude of gratitude that will be the subject of another chapter. Gratitude is an important concept in positive psychology and has been well researched as helpful to our living an abundant life. Treasuring is to savor all the good memories that come to us each and every day. We gain more out of life if we reflect over the good that comes out of each day rather than expanding on the few negatives. Treasuring each day is a positive choice we can make to impact our positive growth. Then the last phrase that stands out to me is "if I ruled the world every head would be held up high". The thought of the importance of personal self esteem and respecting each other's self esteem comes to my mind in this phrase of the lyrics. I will delve more into self esteem in the future. In recent years self esteem has been given a bad rap. We need as we go through each day holding our head up high so we can see the roses in our life, the moon beams in the sky, and the beauty of the sunsets that we can apply to all the good things in life. If we insecurely mope around with our head to the ground we will miss so much of what life has to offer,

Dreams will always stay dreams if we do not go for them. Another favorite dream song is one I look forward to hearing if I am driving down the highway listening to a San Antonio classic rock radio station. The song, "Dreams" by Van Halen has been a favorite since my high school days. I had always liked the energy of the song. As well as, since being a big believer in the importance of dreams, I appreciated the overall theme. I thought to myself that I had never really looked at the lyrics of the song so decided to look for the lyrics and check out videos of the song. You can finds several great videos on Youtube related to this song. I often use this song as a motivator to college students I work with.

From the context of the whole song it is focusing on the dreams of a couple in a relationship who are facing difficult times. "World turns black and white, Pictures in an empty room" causes me think of metaphors for barrenness and despair leading to broken dreams. From dreams in a relationship point of view, I believe the song is saying don't give up. Keep climbing higher and higher to keep hold of shared dreams. It is important in marriage to support each others dreams and to also have united dreams together. In the difficult times the shared dreams can help the couple work together and stay strong on climbing higher in life together.

Looking at the song from just an individual dreamer standpoint, I first notice "reach for the golden ring, . . . and spread your wings."

Go for the gold in your dreams. Not meaning money instead, go for the best for your life in your dreams! Keep going "higher and higher" focuses in on dreaming big. Not every big dream comes true but dreams move us out of the empty black and white of life. They take us out of the empty room. Where do the dreams take us? Sometimes as the one lyric phrase says, "Who knows what we will find?". We often don't know what God has in store as we move out with dreams he has implanted in us. Yet if we don't dream or stay sulking about broken dreams, we will know where we are, as we will remain stuck in the same empty room going nowhere.

"Straight up we will climb" relates to our discipline and perseverance in following our dreams. We again go nowhere if we just write our dream down and stay seated in our recliner. We need to be actively engaged in reaching for the sky and spreading our wings following a plan of action to go for the dream. We have been reminded recently in the political arena discussions that dreamers who actively have reached out for the gold ring have been one reason for America's success. To continue this we need to be dreamers who dream big and then are willing to spread our wings to reach those dreams!

In my work with college students I encourage them at the beginning of the semester to dream big dreams. Life has much to offer if we work hard and go for the dreams and goals we want to accomplish on our life journey. There are also hardships and struggles which at times bring chaos into our lives. At these junctures we often need to re-evaluate our dreams and see if they need changed or new pathways to obtain them

I don't apologize for telling students to think big about their lives. I was reminded about today a quote from C. S. Lewis, "It is not that we desire too much, but that we desire too little. Our appetites are not too big, they are too small." How much more in life could we accomplish if we went big with our dreams for our lives? Often what stops us from dreaming big are life's pains that overtake us as well as worries that keep us bound up in the chaos of life. We don't see our dreams coming true instead life looks like just a chaotic mess of knots and twine. What started me thinking about this recently was remembering the song by Gary Wright back in the 1970's called "Dream Weaver". It was another High School favorite song of mine.

The song reminds me of how I encourage students to follow their dreams. It reminds me of the importance of dreaming big. Some of the words remind me of the famous quote, "Reach for the moon, even if you miss you will land among the stars". This is much better than those who do not try and just trudge the mud of this earth just existing with no aspirations. The Dream weaving concept also made me think that we often have many dreams through out life. Some we reach, some are changed and reworked. When we go through the process of reaching our dreams, life can seem like a mess like the underside of a rug that looks chaotic. But once we accomplish our dream and look back at all the pains and struggles we see how they fit together in a beautiful pattern.

The term Dream Weaver in the song also made me wonder who the Dream Weaver is? Reading a little about Gary Wright his worldview comes across as heavy in Eastern religious thought so the Dream Weaver may be an impersonal force of the universe. From my Christian worldview I see a personal God in Jesus Christ being the Dream Weaver. Therefore I seek to have my dreams for my life line up with God's will and direction for my life. The God of the Bible can use dreams in our lives. Here are just a few references to dreams and visions from the Bible:

And it shall come to pass afterward that I will pour out My Spirit on all flesh; your sons and your daughters shall prophesy, your old men shall dream dreams, your young men shall see visions." Joel 2:28

"And it shall come to pass in the last days, says God, that I will pour out of My Spirit on all flesh; your sons and your daughters shall prophesy, your young men shall see visions, your old men shall dream dreams." Acts 2:17

Then the Spirit took me up and brought me in a vision by the Spirit of God into Chaldea, to those in captivity. And the vision that I had seen went up from me. So I spoke to those in captivity of all the things the Lord had shown me." Ezekiel 11:24-25

". . . the secret was revealed to Daniel in a night vision. So Daniel blessed the God of heaven." Daniel 2:19

In your life take time to think over dreams you have for the next part of your life journey. Desire big dreams in your future. Don't go small. You will be surprised with a little commitment, discipline and hard work what you can accomplish.

I am bringing up to you a lot of songs in this section as I have found so many good songs relate to following dreams. I do hope you take the time to look up each song on Youtube or Vimeo and enjoy the videos as that will add to your own personal reflection on the concepts I am trying to get across. There is a song I always share in my last lecture of a semester with students. I want them to remember that each of them have their own dreams to carry with pride down the highway of life. I want you the reader to understand that as well. The song I share is Jim Croce's song, "*I Got A Name*". Being a dreamer I always enjoyed this song by Jim Croce. He had so many wonderful songs in his short life but this was my favorite.

The song pictures someone with strong self esteem and a deep healthy pride in what his passion—his song is. He is proud of his family name as he looks up to his father. Some may think his passionate dream is foolish but he is willing to take the risk to keep singing it out loud and carrying it with him on down the highway of life. There is a commitment not to give up and to not regret— even if it gets him nowhere. Openness to failure and being human by following the dream is seen in the phrase "If it gets me nowhere, I go there proud". He doesn't want life to pass him by with regrets rather to make the most of life singing his song and living his dream. That makes me think again of John Goddard's story. That is the Living More Than OK life!

The way the years fly by, it is like we are traveling down the highway. We need times on the country paths as well as the highway. Do we want a life where life passes us by or one where we are following our dream? Are we sharing our dream with others? Are we willing to take a risk on our dream with a sense of commitment when others try to dissuade us? Remember to dream big yet on your journey be open to other opportunities

We need to move from our dreams to reaching them by turning our dreams into goals. It is important to write those goals down so we know what we are aiming to achieve in our lives. One book I suggest to students in setting educational and life goals is the book, *Write It Down, Make It Happen*, by Henriette Anne Klauser PhD. She has taught English at several Universities and is a writing and communications consultant to Fortune 500 companies. Her book looks at the importance of writing down your goals for what you really want out of your life. The book is full of stories of famous people and not so famous people who accomplished amazing things in their lives. One common element in them was that they wrote down lists and goals of what they wanted to do. The stories show how the goals they wrote down came true.

One of the first stories she mentions is that of Scott Adams. He is well known as the cartoonist behind the Dilbert comic strip. Scott did not graduate from high school and become a cartoonist right away. His early career life was that of a technology worker. He did at the time have a habit of doodling during work. I do not know if that is a basic skill of a cartoonist. That may explain why I never became one as I do not doodle. Henriette points out Scott Adams did something else. He started a habit of writing 15 times a day, "I will become a syndicated cartoonist." If you know anything about writers and artists rejection is part of their life journey. Scott Adams never gave up, he kept trying by resending the cartoon out to possible vendors.

One day it happened that he received a contract to syndicate the Dilbert Cartoon. That is when he changed what he wrote down. He then started writing "I will be the best cartoonist on the planet."

That is difficult to know who is the best at cartooning but one has to admit he made Dilbert very popular as it became a cartoon listed in newspapers around the world. His Dilbert books have sold well as well as Dilbert fans can buy Dilbert mugs, calendars and other items. All of this from a personal dream, turned into a written down goal list.

As you read through Dr. Klauser's book you can read a variety of stories of personal dreams coming true as people wrote them down in diaries, journals, scraps of paper, or goal statement forms. Is it some kind of magic to write something down and it happens? No I don't believe it is magic. Just writing it down does not mean it will happen. Even though I believe by writing dreams and goals down we are allowing our minds to make a stronger commitment to them.

Another excellent book on the same topic is *Creating Your Best Life*, by Caroline Adams Miller and Dr. Michael Frisch. Their book also is based on years of looking at successful people and researching what made them successful. One common element was that they work down their dream lists and goals. So there is something to this idea of writing down what you want out of life.

There are a couple aspects of writing things down that I believe can help in reaching the goal you are trying for. First of all by writing the goal or desire down you are focusing your mind to work towards the end of reaching your goal. If my mind is more focused I can plan better to reach the goal. A focused mind also allows for stronger levels of persistence. After a couple of rejection letters Scott Adams could have given up his daily writing his "I will become a syndicated cartoonist" list. Then he would have just resigned himself to stop doodling and work quietly in his cubicle. The world would then be a less funny place as Dilbert would have never happened. By writing his list each day he kept focused on not letting the rejection get the best of him. I am not a Dilbert fan but I can say the world is a better place because of Adams humor found in the Dilbert cartoon.

The writing down of your goals also makes you have a higher commitment level. If my goal is just something I talk about to friends it can be just that. Just talk. But if I take the time to write it down I force myself to think through ways of reaching the goal. Writing the goal down makes me take more ownership and responsibility in making the goal happen. If you are trying to accomplish some things that you just keep mulling over in your mind try writing them down. If you need some inspiration in doing this look for the book *Write It Down, Make It Happen* and/ or *Creating Your Best Life* in your local library and read the inspiring stories of people just like you who have accomplished their dreams by writing it down. Remember that to be Living More Than OK it is important to follow your dreams!

Reflections:

Think over a couple of things you really wanted to accomplish this year and are already falling out of your grasp. Take some moments to write them down specifically how you want your goal concretely to look. Try what Scott did and go back that goal every day writing it down and see what happens.

Set aside some free time on a weekend or evening and create your own life dream list. Dream Big about the things you desire to do, places you want to travel to, things you want to learn! If you do Journaling, write your list in your journal, or you may want to make a creative poster of your dream list. Do write it down so you can begin checking your dream items off as you accomplish them.

What would the world be like if you were ruler for a day? What positive choices can you learn from the song, IF I RULED THE WORLD, to brighten your daily journey?

Are you a dreamer or stuck in your recliner in an empty room? Take ten minutes to reflect over a new dream for yourself. Maybe it is to be involved in a new volunteering venture, or writing, or a new business idea, or fill your own blank. If you are in a relationship take time to share your dreams with each other. Discuss shared dreams you want to work on together

Look over your life journey. Was there a dream you had that looking back you can see how the difficulties were well worth the final end result? Looking forward is there an out of this world starry sky dream you want to aim for in the next phase of your life journey? Write it down and plan to go for it.

Resources for further learning:

Adams Miller, Caroline & Friesch, Michael, Creating Your Best Life, Sterling, 1994.
Bennett, Tony, "If I Ruled The World", Songs For the Jet Set—CD.
Croce, Jim, "I Got A Name", I Got A Name—CD.
Goddard, John, The Survivor, Health Communications Inc. 2001.
Kallestad, Walt, Wake Up Your Dreams, Zondervan, 1996.
Keaggy, Phil, "Dream Again, Dream Again—CD, 2006
Klauser, Henriette Anne, Write It Down, Make It Happen, Fireside Books, 2001.
Maxwell, John, Put Your Dreams to the Test, Thomas Nelson, 2011
Van Halen, "Dreams", 5150—CD
Wright, Gary, "Dream Weaver", Dream Weaver—CD, 1992

Walking the Pride and Arrogance Tightrope (Self Esteem)

In the chapter about dreams I spoke of a song by Jim Croce that talks about having pride in oneself. Is having pride a good or a bad thing? Many of us were taught that pride was wrong and a sin. I believe a healthy pride is being assured of who you are and your strengths. It becomes bad when it turns into arrogant narcissism which is an "I am better than you type of attitude".

Part of having a healthy pride is knowing and understanding your personal God given strengths and talents. It is a basis of a strong self-esteem. Self-esteem as a topic has been battered over the recent years because of what I believe is a wrong view of it. Self-esteem isn't about giving everyone getting a trophy. Instead it should be helping individuals to see and understand their own unique strengths and talents. One book that helps us with understanding this is *Making a Difference by Being Yourself* by Gregory E. Huszczo.

One reason I immediately wanted to read this book was that perusing through it, I noticed the author was focusing in on the MBTI, (Myers-Briggs Type Inventory). Although personality inventories have also received a bad rap from some I do believe from taking them and studying them, they do offer helpful insights in understanding ourselves better. The problem is when people are cookie cutter labeled by the personality assessments. Those who truly understand the nature of personality assessments such as the MBTI do not do that. Gregory Huszczo helps in this book to show how the personal insights gleaned by knowing our personality type can help individuals grow in their work relationships and personal relationships.

Think over the phrase "making a difference". In living a life more than ok, having an attitude of making a difference is a motivator to move us beyond just existing. The author brings out in the text, that starting with the desire to make a difference helps in giving meaning and fulfillment to our lives. As he states in the book, "The More we notice opportunities to make a difference and push ourselves to rise to the occasion, the better we will feel about ourselves as well as life in general" (Page 7). Living this way gives our lives meaning and purpose.

The book discusses how making a difference is based on three parts in our life: our abilities, our motivation, and opportunities that come up in our daily lives. The more we know the unique elements of our personality type we can understand how to use our abilities in our interactions to make a difference. The primary realms we can make a difference is in our work and in our relationships. It is all about how we touch other people's lives. That is how we make a difference.

Think over how we can help make a difference. In the book the author gives a list of ways we make a difference in work or relationships to help the reader brain storm other ways they have or can make differences in lives around them. Here are some items from the list: solving a problem, being a role model, motivating others, resolving a conflict, team building, caring for others, reducing stress in a situation. As you consider the list of items you can probably think of other ways of making a difference. To make a difference in these areas we need a strong self-esteem. You can't care about others effectively if you constantly look down on yourself or negatively berate yourself.

As we understand how our unique personality traits work, we can be effective in making a difference. Based on our personality type we all attack problems differently, we care for others differently, we team build differently. The key word is different. Personality is not about right or wrong or being better than another. It is about our unique strengths we each bring to the opportunities in dealing with things in life differently from the next person.

We can only imagine how better life in the world would be if each of us took the viewpoint of making a positive difference in our workplaces and relationships. It would create a more giving environment instead of a passive, "I'm sure someone else will do it" or worse yet, the victim mentality we see too often today of "why doesn't someone help me. It's not fair!". Difference makers seek to improve their own lives and also help other people and situations around them. The positive paradox is that the more we give and serve the more we will find our lives more fulfilled rather than empty.

Another way to have positive pride in ourselves is to listen to what we say to ourselves in our self talk. It is basically the things we say to ourselves in our minds about ourselves. One of the best books I have read speaking on the subject is *From Panic To Power* by Lucinda Bassett. She is the founder of the Midwest Center for Stress and Anxiety. It is a book on anxiety but she looks at self talk from the concept of Compassionate Self-Talk. I am a big believer in the importance of Positive Self-Talk which is the same thing but the term compassionate intrigued me. If we think about it and ponder over the negatives things we say to ourselves we are often more compassionate to others than to ourselves. We can often be our harshest critics. We stop ourselves from progressing in our work or activities we want to do because we put ourselves down. Thoughts such as "someone else could do this better than me"; "there is no way I can be successful with that"; "There are so many better writers, painters, singers, . . . than me". The negative critic inside stops us from what we can really do. If we heard our best friend say these things we would stop them and help them think in a more positive way. But living with our inner self many of us continue to tear ourselves down with negative self-talk.

Ms. Bassett says of compassionate self-talk, "it is any message or dialogue with yourself or someone else that makes you feel good, strong, happy, confident, relaxed, capable, loving, energetic, peaceful or motivated." It is the messages we tell ourselves that can overcome and help us flourish in our daily walk. We need to understand that our thought life is powerful enough to motivate ourselves to do great things, to overcome depression and anxiety, to gain power in difficult times, and to rise above being a passive victim and conquer the difficulties.

We first have to understand the level of our negative self-talk. She recommends carrying a small spiral notebook, (I use these myself—I call these my brain on paper), and when you hear yourself say something negative like, "I feel too blah to go to work today" or "I can't volunteer at the Summer camp, what if I make a fool of myself?" Write the statement down. After a week look over the statements. Is there a theme? Are you a "what ifer"? Such as "what if I fail, what if I look foolish". Funny thing about what ifs is that they rarely come true. Or maybe you're an "I Can'tr" Phrases like "I can't do that" come up over and over again in your self-talk. As you look at the list consider how negative is what you are saying to yourself. How harmful are the statements? How are they defeating you or stopping your success.

In your notebook Ms. Bassett says to rewrite thought replacements. Take the time to write what you should say instead the negative things you are saying. This is like re-writing the scripts for your life. In being compassionate in your rewriting of negative self-talk be realistic. If you are feeling depressed because your car was wrecked don't try to negate a true feeling by saying, "I am not depressed I am cheerful and happy. I am gald my car got totaled." Instead say "I am feeling down about the car but I can be thankful I wasn't hurt." In understanding compassionate thought replacement we need to understand our thoughts can make us bitter or better. They can cause our emotions to spiral down in the dumps or spiral upwards to a energetic triumph over our difficulties.

Since I as a Bookhead am speaking of self-talk I do want to mention another book that echoes what Ms. Bassett speaks of in her book. The book was suggested to me by a Professor at Trinity

Evangelical Divinity School years ago. It is *What To Say When You Talk To Yourself,* by Dr. Shad Helmstetter. He goes more in-depth into the topic of self-talk than Ms. Bassett. Dr. Helmstetter is also very practical on improving self-talk and critical thinking to help individuals live a better life.

One place our self-esteem level affects us is in our work life. With work taking up a large amount of our daily living I am always interested in how to keep work moving at a more than ok level. So I was intrigued at coming upon a book entitled, *Happiness At Work: Maximizing your Psychological Capital for Success* by Jessica Pryce-Jones. I want to look at a concept in her chapter on Confidence concerning Self-Belief; as this relates to having a healthy pride in ourselves. Another term for this is self efficacy.

Self efficacy is the internal feelings and beliefs we hold about we how can do at different tasks and knowledge. How capable do we believe we are. Albert Bandura the noted Psychologist known for his work on self efficacy defines it this way," *self-efficacy is the belief in one's capabilities to organize and execute the courses of action required to manage prospective situations."* This is our capacity to believe in ourselves which is important in our work life to make the most out of our time in the workplace. If we believe in our ability our work will flow much easier and we will have higher levels of satisfaction in what we are doing. It is also an impetus to keep us growing in our skills.

A big enemy of our self-efficacy is "I can'titus". It is the internal thought sickness that tells us we can't perform as well as others. I can't do this project. I can't be creative in my work. The I cant's bring stress to our work and drags out each work day. That is when the ball and chain feeling begins to overtake us.

By building up our self belief we can have more success on the job as we will reach our goals and perform better on our projects we do at work. We will be able to expand our possibilities more at work by creatively seeing new ways to help clients and customers. Creativity and skills levels grow when we have a positive belief about our capabilities. This allows us then a higher level of happiness in our work.

Some things that can build our self efficacy levels are to keep growing in our work skills. I can chant all day long that I believe that I am a great with my computer skills. Yet if all I know about the computer is how to push the power button my self belief statements are to no avail.

So be a lifelong learner, attend workshops, read up on journals and research in your work field. Attend conferences that relate to your work. Keep persistent in the difficulties of your work until you reach success. Don't have a give up attitude but a keep on going and growing attitude. Learn from other co-workers. Don't be an island, instead appreciate what others who work with you are doing, Also learn more about self efficacy to build up your levels of it. Check out on the web informational articles there on this important subject of self-efficacy.

Our beliefs affect our job performance and the quality of our work experience. We work about 80,000 hours in our lifetime so we should want to make the most of that time instead of dreading that time. So it is important to build up our self-efficacy and self-esteem.

I am a strong believer in lifelong learning not for just our career life development as it adds to our quality of life the Living More Than OK life. Through continued learning we keep improving ourselves building our skills and self-esteem. A sensible level of pride tells us to keep learning and growing. It is arrogance that tells us "I know it all so I do not need to learn from anyone else!" One way I enjoy learning is that I enjoy learning at conferences. One time I attended the National Career Development Association Global conference in San Antonio. I appreciate that our work and personal life is enlivened beyond boredom if we are taking time to learn new ideas from others. That is the main importance for my going to conferences.

One topic at that conference that stood out to me first came from a keynote speaker, Mark Guterman of Meaningful Careers. Their website is MeaningfulCareers.com The topic of his presentation was "In Remembrance Lies the Secret . . . Lessons From The Past Guiding Us Into The Future". He touched on a number of ideas yet the driving point that spoke to me was that we are impacted by the people in our past. Our families, close friends, and role models have an impact on how we shape our values for what we want to pursue in our work world and personal world.

I like quotes that speak a kernel of truth to me and one that stood out in Mr. Guterman's presentation was by David Brooks, "We inherit a great river of knowledge, a flow of patterns coming from many sources, none of us exist self made in isolation from it." We each are where we are at partly because of choices and responses to those in our past who have interacted with and impacted our lives.

We need to take quiet times aside, to savor the impact that those in our past, have had on the development of our present state in this journey we each are on. We need to take time and think through how past advice and personal examples have helped to shape our present. Through appreciation and gratitude for their impact, this can help us move towards a more positive future. I know my life has been moved to excel and change direction do to wise advice from others who I respected in the past.

After the Keynote speaker I found it interesting as I was looking at the afternoon speakers, there was a session on "Discover The Impact Of Our Past By Learning How To Use Career Genograms". A genogram is a graphing or mapping tool to look at your family tree. Since I am a strong believer in savoring the past for what we can learn from it, I could not pass this session up.

I was somewhat familiar with Genograms (These are a pictorial or graph of a person's familial history often going back three generations). The genograms can give us insight into how we are living our lives in relation to our past family interactions. I must say I had never looked at them from the career standpoint. So this was refreshing to learn new ways to use Genograms. In some case studies reviewed in the session, I could see why people went the career direction they went in relation to past family members careers. In discussion and sharing in the session others pointed out that it is also a helpful tool maybe not to predict a particular career path, but to help people understand how their career values were shaped.

Both of these conference sessions helped me to see the importance of the past in our life journey. I often tell people we cannot change the past. But that day at the conference I gained a better understanding of how we can learn from the past to make better present choices. If you would like to learn more about Genograms check out the website www.genograms.org and try doing one.

As I end this chapter even though I believe self-talk is important. Life is more than talk. For the arrogant prideful person life is always about talk, but sensible useful pride goes beyond that to hard work. When I speak to my Student Success course students, about the power of our self-talk, I tell them we have to move beyond our positive self-talk. Changing our negative thoughts to positive is helpful but with no working action nothing will be accomplished. We need to actively work out our positive thoughts for progress to occur in our dreams, or profitable changes we want for our lives. The book of Proverbs 14:23 tells us, *"All hard work brings a profit, but mere talk leads only to poverty."*

Let's say for example, my self-talk is about getting in better physical shape. I may say things like, "I am going to exercise to improve my health for my self and to be a better me for my family." I even go so far as ordering a Leslie Sansone DVD to do walking at home. Then if all I do is sit in my recliner stuffing cupcakes in my face while I watch the DVD, is that going to help me get in better physical condition? No, I have to rise up from the chair and start walking, go outside for a jog, or join a health club if the recliner is too much of a temptation.

Another example I use with my students, many who struggle with Math, I suggest they can change their self-talk from, "I am no good at math-I just can't do it." to "I need to pass Algebra I to receive my degree, so even though I don't love Math I will do whatever it takes to pass it." What is the *"doing whatever it takes"*? The student needs to work on going to tutoring, place extra time in his schedule to increase the number of math problems he practices. For those students struggling with math I tell then when they start dreaming of numbers chasing them in their dreams they are probably doing the right number of math problems in their personal study time.

What I am getting at, is once your self-talk has been changed into a positive mode you need to jump into active work on what you want for yourself. Here is a helpful quote from Napoleon Hill: *"Do not wait; the time will never be "just right'. Start where you stand, and work with whatever tools you may have at your command, and better tools will be found as you go along."* When we need to make a change, it is easier to make excuses and stay stuck in the soft comfort of the recliner with remote in hand. Waiting for the right time to change will not work, as time will eventually pass us by and the positive changes for possibilities in our life will pass us by. I know from past experience in my life. I like how Napoleon Hill says to start with the tools you have at your disposal to get moving. Again move away from the excuses of waiting for the "right"—time, people, circumstances, or God. I love the God excuse. Mind you, as a Christian, I do believe in seeking God's guidance, but many times sitting around waiting to hear from God, is a cop-out to keep from moving into the tough work of action. Seriously, the move from positive thinking to the hard work of action is tough but necessary. As we take the first step with the tools we have available more helpful tools will come our way as we progress in our journey toward what we want.

Sometimes as we are working hard at accomplishing what we want, we begin to be tired and want to give up. A reality check reminds us that hard work is called hard work for a reason. It is hard and difficult at times. When you are ready to give up, think over these ten positive benefits to hard work in our lives. Use them as reminders why you need to keep pressing on, working for the changes in your life. They come from the book Life's Greatest Lessons by Hal Urban:

1. *Hard work helps us realize our potential.*
2. *Hard work helps us face up to life.*
3. *Hard work makes us feel good.*
4. *Hard work builds character.*
5. *Hard work earns the respect of others.*
6. *Hard work earns self-respect.*
7. *Hard work adds meaning.*
8. *Hard work gets the best results.*
9. *Hard work becomes a habit.*
10. *Hard work is healthy.*

So in closing this chapter know that there is nothing wrong with having a healthy self-pride in your unique strengths and talents. At the same time realize the world isn't just about you. We are given talents to help our fellow man on their journeys. Otherwise we turn into boastful narcissists. Do not be just talkers about yourself be doers in the hard work of being the best you possible. Begin working today on improving your Living More Than OK!

Reflections:

Write down on a piece of paper several examples of when you have made a difference at work. Then Write down on a piece of paper several examples of when you have made a difference in personal relationships. Think over these times. How did they make you feel? How did these experiences affect those around you and yourself in a positive manner?

Spend 15 minutes thinking over your most recent thoughts from the past few days. Jot down a few of the negative scripts you say to yourself. Imagine you heard your best friend saying these same things. What would you tell your friend out of a spirit of compassion to help them say things that are more positive? Be more compassionate to yourself!

On a scale of 1–10 one being low and 10 high what is your level of self-belief about your work capabilities. Journal about a growth area you can improve on in your work life. Take the time to go to on the web and read up on self-efficacy.

Try doing a Genogram going back to your grandparents on both your mother and father's sides. Reflect over their lives. What do you remember or even think about family myths about relatives? Jot down in a diary or journal how your values and life experiences have been shaped by them.

Resources for further learning:

Bassett, Lucinda, From Panic To Power, Harper Collins.

Helmstetter, Shad, What To Say When You Talk To Yourself, Pocket Books, 1990.

E. Huszczo, Gregory, Making a Difference by Being Yourself, Nicolas Brealey Publishing, 2010.

Pryce-Jones, Jessica, Happiness At Work: Maximizing Your Psychological Capital for Success, Wiley, 2010.

Urban, Hal Life's Greatest Lessons, Touchstone, 2003.

Don't Stay On The Mat—Bounce Back With Resilience

Sometimes as positive as we desire to be, life just knocks us down to the mat. There are just some things we cannot control such as sickness, accidents, or on the job front—corporate downsizings. The good news is we do not have to stay on the mat. That is where resilience comes in for helping us move forward in living more than ok. The definition of resilience is an ability to recover from or adjust easily to misfortune or change.

Dr. Karen Reivich and Dr. Andrew Shatte in their book *The Resilience Factor* show their in-depth research on resilience in people's lives. They state that the primary obstacle to people bouncing back to life's knockdowns, "is not genetics, not childhood experiences, not a lack of opportunity or wealth. The principle obstacle is tapping into our inner strength lies with our cognitive style, which we'll refer in this book as thinking style." (pg 11). There is that word thinking again. You may want to re-read the chapter on critical thinking. So often the liberal media tries to reduce all our life problems down to the externals so unthinking people believe only the government can solve our problems with more services. Yet the real solution comes internally within each and every person.

I once received an email comment on a blog post I did entitled "Our Humanity Messiness and Choices". The person rightly pointed out that some messes occur due to our being locked up by our holding onto false beliefs generated through culture, society, religion, family, and ect. The commenter then used the example that men often do not go for help with problems due to the false beliefs that they should be strong and figure it out by themselves. This is a false pride in self, which is only fear of breaking free from the belief controlling them. The email ended with stating victory in the power to choose to free oneself of the fears of false belief. So I wanted to look more at our power to choose and think as it relates so well with the resilience needed to bounce back from life's difficulties.

We can face fewer false beliefs if we challenge them with Critical Thinking_skills I mentioned earlier in this book. Improving our critical thinking is a choice we each must make. I mentioned power along with choice. "The greatest power that a person possesses is the power to choose" J. Martin Kohe, (author and psychologist). We have amazing power for good possibilities and bad in our lives based on the choices we make. Hal Urban_in his book *Life's Greatest Lessons* says, ". . . we all have the potential to do more with our lives. Every human being is capable of making great strides in self development and major increases in achievements." As I have mentioned before that is a driving force in initially starting my blog and now this book—the desire to help people maximize their potential and possibilities in life.

Too many people fail to reach their potential because they feel they do not have control. They fail to see that each day is full of choices that affect our present and futures. Sure there are the flat tires that come in our lives. No one wakes up choosing to be stranded on the side of the road with a flat. Even then we make a choice to get out of the car to fix the flat or call Triple A to fix the flat for us. Happenstance happens. Yet when the stuff of life we cannot control come crushing in we still have a choice what to do in response. Even the response of allowing ourselves to be crushed by the circumstance is a choice. Being crushed by life events is not a fun thing. Been there, been crushed, and don't recommend remaining crushed for a length of time. It is very depressing.

One story I have been using with College students recently on bouncing back with resilience, is the life of Dr. C. Moorer. He writes in his autobiography, *From Failure to Promise: An Uncommon Path to Professoriate,* the honest story of his dreams of going to college to be an engineer to then flunking out after his first year. His is a powerful story of growing up in the ghetto areas of Detroit. He did well in school due to hard work and parents of Christian faith who instilled in him values to do his best. Yet he admits the public schools of Detroit did not prepare him well for college and that was one factor of many that caused him to flunk out. What is refreshing about his story there is no victim mentality of the blame game. He took ownership of his failure then pressed onto go back to school up to earning his doctorate. Hard work and his personal religious faith pushed him forward to his goal.

To maximize our living we need to see the positive choices we can make each day. As I read Dr. Moorer's story I saw his choices that molded his life story. Even to make lemonade out of the lemons that drop into our lives. One of my favorite Psychological theories, (probably because I believe in the power of Choice), is *Choice Theory* by Dr. William Glasser. A central aspect of Choice Theory is the belief that we are internally, not externally motivated. While other theories suggest that outside events "cause" us to behave in certain predictable ways, Choice Theory teaches that outside events never "make" us to do anything. What drives our behavior are internally developed notions of what is most important and satisfying to us. Another major concept in Choice Theory is the notion that we always have some choice about how to behave. This does not mean that we have unlimited choice or that outside information is irrelevant as we choose how to behave. It means that we have more control than some people might believe and that we are responsible for the choices we make. What is going on internally in us is more important than the externals that affect our life journey. The quality of our thinking is what is most important, which goes back to the importance of critical thinking. We are responsible to make the best choices for our good and for those traveling on the journey with us.

For example, I have a flat tire and simply ignore it and keep driving. "My what is the problem with this road? The road sure seems to be bumpy!" I say to myself. Of course it is not the road condition—it is the flat tire. If I ignore the external, the small problem of the flat tire turns into the big problem of a smashed rim and broken axle. That bigger problem was the result of my ignoring the small problem. So by understanding the power of our choices we can maximize our living and sidetrack many of our problems which are results of poor choices or choosing not to choose.

As you wake up each day understand that you, not others are in control of your choices. Make the choice to make choices that will be the best for your life journey and for those travelling with you. "It is the big choices we make that set our direction. It is the smallest choices we make that get us to the destination." (Shad Helmstetter). By making positive quality choices we can bounce back in a positive way from much of the negative consequences and situations that bombard our lives.

Resilience causes us to want more than just existing in life? People become trapped in mediocrity living the sameness of what I think of as a Ground Hog Movie day life. I don't know if you have ever seen that movie if not make it a point to see as it is an eye opener about how many of us respond to the day to day grind of life. Doing the same thing over and over again. Waking up, going to work and watching the same dull tv shows or lame internet videos. Do we dare to try for something more?

The fear of the scariness in trying something new keeps us from stepping out into a new direction. We become out of touch with our dreams and passions. We can even become so downcast to think, "Maybe I don't deserve better." The issue is we deserve the best life possible. There are many things we can do to enrich and grow our lives and new possibilities for our futures.

Choices and right thinking is part of resilience that overcomes the fear of the status quo in our life journey. I want here to bring up a chorus of a song I heard once that relates to the openness for change that is important to growth in life. The chorus is from a song Maybe by The Sick Puppies that I heard on the radio one day. There is so much more in the song so you may want to search for it on-line and listen to the whole song. But for this discussion on resilience let's just focus on the chorus right now:

> "Maybe it's time to change, And leave it all behind, I've never been one to walk alone, I've always been scared to try, So why does it feel so wrong
>
> To reach for something more, To wanna live a better life, What am I waiting for?
>
> 'Cause nothing stays the same, Maybe it's time to change."

Thinking over what is being said in the song, we do not have to resign ourselves to a hopeless life. We can rise above the fear and aim for a better life. It all starts with a thoughtful choice. Step out with the dreams we have been given inside to go for new directions in our life pathway. We need to trust ourselves as we take that first step towards change.

Jesus often challenged people to make changes and not look back, as He said in Luke 9:2, "No one who puts his hand to the plow and looks back is fit for service in the kingdom of God." Another line says, "And maybe it's time to change, And leave it all behind". We don't always have to forget the past. But if it is something negative that you are holding on to and stopping you from a better life it is best to let it go. Then you are free to move on to that better life. Take some time to think over the reflection questions and move into some changes that will give you a better life!

Another way to look at Resilience is that part of our being that keeps us going during the tough times. When we want to give up our resilience level is that inner voice that says "don't give up keep moving forward and upward." It helps us to bounce back when life throws us unexpected curveballs. We can through planning and goal setting control much of what life throws at us but we can't control everything. Resilience can give us the strength to keep plodding along the path instead of giving up.

We each have different difficulties on our journeys to test our resilience. In dealing with these difficulties part of resilience is knowing our limits and knowing when we need to ask for help. There is nothing wrong in asking for help. That help can come from our fellow travelers on life's journey or Divine help as we call out to God for help. Because sometimes we need to be humble and knowledgeable of our strengths and weaknesses, to know when we need to ask for help. Here is a portion of a song Strong Enough, by Matthew West that looks at the need to be open to a higher power when we just don't have the strength to carry on:

> "I know I'm not strong enough to be, everything that I'm supposed to be
>
> I give up, I'm not strong enough, Hands of mercy won't you cover me
>
> Lord right now I'm asking you to be, Strong enough, Strong enough
>
> For the both of us Well maybe, Maybe that's the point, To reach the point of giving up Cause when I'm finally, Finally at rock bottom, Well that's when I start looking up, And reaching out"

The song reminded me of difficult days in Chicago after my mother had died, then shortly thereafter the next year, my oldest brother was diagnosed with cancer. He passed away months afterwards, wasting away to nothing in his final days. During that time of grief the company I worked for was taken over by another company. The stress of that time brought me to a depressive collapse. Those were depressing days where like the song says I was at the point of giving up. This was a time when I felt my resilience levels could not cope. I felt the strength of Christ by close friends at church filling in the gap and help from going to a Counselor helped so I did not hit rock bottom. Also by holding onto the promises of God's Word helped me to keep forward on the journey.

The Matthew West song also reminded me of my volunteer work with a drug rehab center in Brownsville, Texas. Their groups used the 12 step program of Alcoholic Anonymous. If you work with addicts you learn from their stories they had to hit rock bottom as the song lyric states, before seeking help. They will admit their turn around was only from God's hand of grace reaching down to pull them up.

Maybe you are facing difficulties now—economic, health, broken relationships. Know that whatever you are facing you need to be open to know your limitations and reach for help. Maybe it is calling a friend to let them know what you are facing. Possibly you need to reach out to your local church or parish for help in finding a Counselor therapist to work for solutions.

Resilience is also about our attitude we carry in our mindset about life. That attitude that guides our inner ability that helps when we are at a seemingly dead-end; to not give up but to keep on going by finding a new way—yes a new attitude. We all at one time or another have life events that drive our emotions to the extremes of hot or cold. Events, where, we come to a dead end. Maybe it is a dream we had where the tables are now turned and we see a nightmare instead. It may be a relationship or a job that has fallen through. At those times we are so low as to feel in our attitude that there is no way to proceed. The failure is too much and the wires that energize are life have been short circuited. We can let worries take over and have a negative attitude that everything is out of control so we better give up on life. That is the picture I see from the beginning of the song. The sad thing is that some people choose to live in the bad dream of their nightmare attitude for the rest of their lives.

The good news is that times of failure do not make us failures for life. We can choose a new attitude. There is even a song that was popular years ago called "New Attitude" by Patti Labelle. We can look at the failure and seek to learn lessons to improve and change our dreams and goals. We have been created to be resilient and move forward from dead-ends with new attitudes. In the song there is the phrase "I tidied up my point of view" it is an important phrase. To bounce back from failure and troubles we need to do an attitude check and reevaluate our next play in the game of life. I like how the song also says a new attitude affects us "from my head to my toes". Our positive attitude change has to affect our whole being to be successful.

On the issue of control we can never be fully in control. But in an attitude check, we need to look at what we can control and change for the better and prayerfully leave what we can't control up to God. In doing this we keep worries to a limit and can keep moving forward with the positive energy we see this song is about. A new attitude gives us a positive feeling about the direction in which we are then moving. So if you are going through difficulties that have brought your attitude to a new low. Take some time for an attitude check and make a choice to change it from your head to your toes.

Resilience reminds us that Positive psychology and spirituality principles are not about us living a carefree life with happy smiles plastered on our face continually. The reality of our life journey, places us in hardships and times of sorrow from time to time. Some of us have more hardships than others. Some of us have higher mountains to climb and lower valleys to go into. The good news is we don't have to stay in the dark valleys or remain on the arduous climb up the mountain. We can have times of exhilarating joy on the mountain top or restful joy in the valley meadows by still flowing streams of refreshing delight. The concept of positive psychology principles is to help people have more joy in their journey as they move out of times of grief and sorrow.

A song that comes to mind on this topic is "Tears of Joy" by Tuck and Patti. It is a simple song with a pleasant jazz feel and joyful energy. Take a listen to it by searching for videos of it on the web. You will be glad you did. The song starts off looking at the reality of life. There are times of sorrow and we can often see it visibly in people's countenances. Some of those times are so full of deep grief they leave scars that time can not erase. We can move beyond the time of grief but sometimes there are physical scars or emotional ones that on certain times of the year trigger memories of the person or event. I know that is true in my life as there are days of the year when I can remember some of the difficulties I faced or important people that passed away.

When dealing with friends or family going through times of sorrow it is important to listen to the phrase, "I'm coming to you gently". In sorrow people need the caring presence of others not glib "You'll get over it" or "The Bible says all things work out good!". In the depths of sorrow the individual is not ready to see any good in the situation. In the midst of the confusion of these times in our life there is time to set time aside, and to settle down and rest. It is then that we can feel the presence of the One who loves us. I capitalized the word One as for me in my spiritual worldview, I look at it as being open to experiencing God's presence during difficult times. I do not know if that is what the song writer meant. Holding on to God in difficult times has been a great help to me in the times of sorrow I have experienced.

Now what about the promise made in the song, "Beside of every tear that sorrow has left you Tears of joy will take their place". What does that mean? It probably means something different to every person reading this. I remembered in Brownsville after a hurricane would pass by with the stormy rains a clear sunny day would come. Many times after a hard rain storm there is joy in seeing a rainbow. This can become a metaphor for the harsh reality of our difficulties in life. After times of tearful sorrow, tears of joy can come into our life. The time period is different for all of us. The songwriter uses tears of joy to move in to wash us clean. As we move into the phase from sorrow to joy we experience a refreshing of our spirits as they have been cleansed. We are then set free from the chains that sorrows bind us with. Free to live with joy on the journey. Again remembering on those certain days memories will come but in the renewed freedom even those days of remembrance can be celebration of what the person meant to us if it was a time of grief. Or if it was a disaster that affected us, the days of remembrance can be a time to reflect on what we learned to improve ourselves through the experience.

Speaking about going through difficult times, in the past year I found myself reading a book *Godforsaken* by Dinesh D'Souza. What I like most about his books is he makes me think about my viewpoint on topics. He is another example of a great critical thinker. I find him reaffirming most of what I believe and sometimes challenging me to think in new ways. The subtitle of the book is "Bad Things Happen. Is there a God who cares? Yes. Here's proof". Just as the song "Tears of Joy" looked at suffering and difficulty this book digs deeper into the subject.

Dr. D'Souza leaves no stone of suffering unturned. He looks at terrible acts of God in nature: earthquakes, hurricanes, tornadoes. Pain and suffering in the animal kingdom which often makes us wonder why God created a nature full of pain and struggle? Of course there is also much human suffering in young people who die too young. People who become paralyzed due to illness and accidents. He discusses the full range of suffering along all spectrums, as these are all areas where people look at the pain and suffering and ask where is God? How can there be a God that allows all this suffering? In my younger years I read the atheist, Bertrand Russell's writings and in recent years I have read the new atheists writings of Dawkins, Hitchens and Harris as well as others. Suffering is one angry complaint they hold up as evidence,(?), that God does not exist. So from that point alone it is important to look at the subject of suffering. Also it is important for me as a Christian to see what there is to learn from suffering.

I appreciate how the book does not describe the suffering in a detached intellectual way but delves into the emotional impact of it in our lives. I remember recently a dear friend in Chicago lost his son to an early death from sickness. When I had received the email from his mother I was shocked as I could not believe what had happened and felt sadness for a dear friend who had been a big help to me when I lived in Chicago. Those sudden unexpected deaths are often the hardest to take in trying to understand the silence of God in it all.

There are too many things I learned from the book to address here is this chapter so as a Bookhead I encourage you to pick up the book in your favorite bookstore or library. But I will touch on a few items. One item that first comes to mind is his discussion on atheism and what he terms "wounded theism". I had always wondered to myself why do these atheists in their writings write full of anger raging against God who they happen to believe does not exist? So you don't believe in God—big deal—get on with your life. In many of them though is a background of religious upbringing and they had become disillusioned. The idea of at the root of their anger at God is a wounded theism makes sense so I can understand where many of them are coming from. Some of them are angry with God so then make a choice to believe in an atheistic faith.

Another point I appreciated was that one purpose of suffering is to help mold us to be more empathic in our caring for others going through suffering. A helpful quote where I forget where I heard it but it is very true. is, "Happiness is an incompetent instructor; much of the knowledge we get in life comes from hardship." As I look back on my life as I went through a very difficult time a friend asked me what was I going to learn from the experience. Through pain and suffering we can either become bitter or become better. I try to aim for the better mindset as the bitter attitude causes a negative spiral downwards. A move to improve to be better, spirals us upwards to an improved attitude and better future response to difficulties.

We should never wish harm and pain on others. My desire in my writings, are to attempt to improve people's happiness and life fulfillment levels. Yet our journey on this earth gives each of us our times of trials and pain. My worldview causes me to turn to God and know He will not forsake me. He is there in the storm with me. Just as Christ suffered more than any of us could imagine there is a promise of a future hope of a world without pain and suffering. An atheist may think I am crazy for believing that. But as I was reading Dr. D'Souza's book verses from Romans 8:19-22 came to mind, "For the creation waits in eager expectation for the children of God to be revealed. [20] For the creation was subjected to frustration, not by its own choice, but by the will of the one who subjected it, in hope [21] that[a] the creation itself will be liberated from its bondage to decay and brought into the freedom and glory of the children of God. [22] We know that the whole creation has been groaning as in the pains of childbirth right up to the present time."

I simply believe the Bible's message of the Fall of man and subsequent fall of nature and the promise of God's love and redemption through Christ makes the most sense out of what I observe in the world around me and in the world's history. That is my belief, yes and I stand firm on that. Just as the atheist stands firm in their faith belief, that this magnificent miraculous world just poofed into existence by random chance.

Again I state resilience is about us being responsible to bounce back from difficulties. We have the choice to just lay there on the mat immobilized or to pick ourselves up and start moving. I was once preparing for my new semester of Teaching a Foundations for College Success course by looking over the new textbook, On Course by Skip Downing the college was using. One chapter that jumped out to me was on Personal Responsibility. We live in an era where it is rare for people to accept responsibility. This is even seen on the governmental level instead of working on problems the leaders point to excuses away from themselves as to why the country is in the mess it is.

It is easier to make up excuses and point to others as the root of our problems than to do the hard work of solving our problems ourselves. The author Skip Downing said this of personal responsibility, "The essence of personal responsibility is responding wisely to life's opportunities and challenges, rather than waiting passively for luck or other people to make the choices for us." Those two key words responding versus waiting have a big impact on how we respond to life.

Skip Downing places people in two categories in relation to responsibility. One is the Victim role. The victim is the waiting passively person. As life events occur and often trouble occur they wait and then blame others for their difficulties. They want a handout or someone such as the government to take care of them. The other role is the Creator role. This person actively responds to find personal solutions. At times they may seek out help from government but on a short term basis, as they ultimately want to be responsible for their own way in life. The passive victim often spirals down to deeper despair and complains about how they got the short end of the stick or how unlucky they are. The Active responder creator instead spirals up with a positive attitude that the difficulty is only a temporary set back and they will bounce back. This is a key element in resilient people of having a comeback attitude.

In both cases a central element is the choices each person makes. The Creator makes positive choices to actively make their lives better. On the other hand the Victim makes choices to passively wait for someone else to help them which creates more hardship. Elisabeth Kuler-Ross said this of choices, "I believe that we are solely responsible for our choices, and we have to accept the consequences of every deed, word, and thought throughout our lifetime." I always emphasize to my students that all our life is made up of continual choices and each choice we make creates a consequence. The creator accepts responsibility for their choices while the victim sits crying unfair and blaming others for their situation. At the end of our life we will look back and realize our life was the result of all our choices.

To have the best life possible we need to be actively engaged in making wise responsible choices. Sad to say our country's culture is moving more and more towards a victim mentality. We need to choose whether we want to be a victim and spiral down in negatively or be a creator and spiral upwards with a positive attitude. Now granted rain and storms occur in every person's life. And there are some who have more storms than others. The creators keep bouncing back resiliently from the storms knowing that there is more to life than just storms. They work at improving their lives and helping others along the way. The victims often stay stuck in the storm and miss the rainbow by staring at the grey clouds in the distance. They also tend to drag others down with them. The choice is up to each of us.

By being responsible we are taking charge of making changes in our lives. Change is one thing we can always count on in life. Sometimes it comes fast and swift and other times change sneaks up on us. Change also varies in that it can be a good change that we can be grateful for or a bad change that negatively impacts our life. As a new semester was starting for my teaching at the college I found myself thinking about change. I found myself pulling off my bookshelf a book I had read years ago, You Can Excel In Times Of Change by Dr. Shad Helmstetter. A few of his ideas on how we can make the most of change in our lives impacted my thinking on this topic of bouncing back with a resilient spirit. The important part of change is how we react. All change has an impact on our lives either bringing good feelings or debilitating us. Loss especially in death of a loved one is a change that is hard to let go of. Especially when the death is unexpected—the change of having that person gone can create a shock that is difficult to overcome. In the same vein job loss is a difficult change to overcome. There is a sense of life is not fair that can take over and hold people in responding to the change by negatively keeping stuck in the pain.

Dr. Helmstetter in this book brings out that many of the changes that occur in our lives when we look at the causation, is often out of our control. But the outcome of the change is controlled by our choices to be responsible in the face of change or irresponsible and staying stuck. He brings out the point that people who make it a habit of being responsible in their lives handle changes better. Those who hold on to excuses and blame often stay stuck longer or go backwards when faced with change.

A key element in our response to change is our attitude. Again we may not be in control of the change agent that affected our life. In response, though we have a choice to shape our attitude in a positive or negative way. Our attitude is a powerful force we can control to make good come from even the worst changes that may occur. Successful people and people who overcome great odds when their lives are examined; their success comes back to the positive attitude they carry in their life.

To excel and take charge of change Dr. Helmstetter encourages the reader to go beyond attitude to change your perception to the resulting future of your choices about the change. Write down and create mental pictures of the next steps in your life journey beyond the change. List the positive things that you want to move towards. Create goals to go after what you want to gain for a better life. If this is not done he says we can stay stuck in what he calls just an average life, just ok. Not a life that is succeeding.

Dr. Helmstetter gives a couple of examples of what he is getting at. He describes a couple that move their mother-in-law in with them with an initial attitude to get to know her better. But in not moving beyond attitude they begin to resent her being there and life turns negative. A young woman takes French classes with an attitude to learn so as to travel to Europe. She never goes beyond the initial attitude and never travels. She keeps a nagging regret of why she took the classes in the first place. So there needs to be a choice to move beyond being stuck by changes. A choice is needed to move beyond living just average or what I call living more than ok.

Just One Victory by Todd Rundgren is a great song looking at the issue of Resilience. There are thoughts of battling with weakness and struggles in life. With true perseverance and prayin' there is no sign of giving up or giving in. As you search for the video of the song and listen to it think of how it relates to resilience. I like some of the powerful analogies in the song.

From the beginning phrase "We've been waiting so long We've been waiting for the sun to rise and shine" along with other phrases; "We've been so downhearted, we've been so forlorn" "We get weak and we want to give in". I see the picture of people going through struggles, cancer, addictions, and depressions make people feel this way. The sense of waiting, and wondering if the sun will ever shine again in their lives. I have had those times in my life. I believe those going through the grief process of losing a loved one can find encouragement in this song. Any of these struggles make the person going through them think with a forlorn heart, "Is it worth going on??" "Maybe I should just give up and give in?"

That is where I appreciate the football analogy is in the song—"We get weak and we want to give in But we still need each other if we want to win Hold that line, baby, hold that line Get up boys and hit 'em one more time We may be losing now but we can't stop trying So hold that line, baby, hold that line." Those lines made me reminisce back to high school days back in Barberton, Ohio being in the marching band during football season. I could visualize in my mind the crowd shouting, "Hold That Line, Hold that line." Think of the analogy. If a football team is down by two touchdowns at halftime, does the coach tell the team during the break, "Boys, you look pretty tired and we are behind. Let's just give up and call it a night. I will tell the other coach we give up. There was a good movie on TV I wanted to see anyway!" No way! He motivates them with "The time has come to take the bull by the horns . . ." and "we still need each other if we want to win". "We need just one victory at the beginning of the second half to get us going now go do it!!!" When going through life struggles we need to be our own coaches giving that kind of a pep talk. It also helps if you surround yourself with friends that can give you that kind of pep talk as well. The key to resilience is to keep on fighting for that victory!

We need to be disciplined and do our part, but as you know from my Christian worldview, I believe there is a spiritual element to our battles. I do not know if Todd Rundgren meant it this way, but with my spirit colored glasses I want to point out a few spiritual ideas I see in the song to consider. From the very beginning I see it with the phrase, "We've been waiting for the sun to rise and shine. Shining still to give us the will." Granted physical sunny days can brighten our moods but does the physical sun give us the will to go on. From my view the Son, Jesus Christ, gives me the will to go on through the battle or struggle. Of course to someone else reading this book the phrase may relate to another spiritual force. I am just stating where I come from with my personal worldview.

The same spiritual idea for me is found later in the song, "You can pull it through if you need to And if you believe it's true, it will surely happen Shining still to give us the will" If you believe it is true makes me think of the principle of faith and belief that is vital for our relationship and walk with God. The light of the Son continues to shine to give us the will to continue the fight. Right after those phrases is the phrase "Prayin for it all day". Prayer is an instrument to being resilient in life's trials for those who believe in a spiritual side to this life journey. We need to work hard for the victory and pray hard for the victory.

The last spiritual element I wish to point out is his mention of the Golden Rule early in the song. Todd Rundgren says, "Take the golden rule, as the best example" as to show us how to act as we fight through the struggle we may be facing. It is not do whatever it takes to win, instead it is act in an ethical manner. In Mathew 7:12 Jesus states, "So in everything, Do to others, what you would have them do to you, for this sums up the law and the prophets." Living that life helps us keep relationships strong through the difficulties of life. Words are easy—it is the actions that are important.

In the end how we deal with our life struggles comes down to our choice as Rundgren states in the song, "I am here to tell you I have made my choice." To gain that just one victory we need to make the choice not to give up in the middle of the game. We each need to make our winning choices as we face the difficulties of life.

Ending this chapter I want to look at a couple real life examples that show resilience in people's lives. Because resilience, is all about not staying on the mat but getting back up when we are knocked down. Each of us in life face hardships that come our way. The hardships come in varying degrees of difficulty. Each one of us face different hardships: job loss, loved ones dying, affairs, divorce, relationship breakups, illnesses, harsh weather events, (tornadoes and hurricanes), accidents, and tragedies such as random shootings. These are negative happenstance events that no one plans for. At least no one I know plans and desires tragedies in their lives.

When we are hit by hardships are emotions are overwhelmed. We feel like the world is crushing us. This happens due to the shock value of the event happening without our full expectation of it. Granted some things such as divorces, job loss, and deaths from long term illnesses are not sudden shocks but still the pain of sadness, depression and anxiety has a strong impact on us.

One example comes from a person I know and respect, who lives in Chicago who has an amazing resilience story. Her name is Karla Fioni. She has told her story in a memoir entitled, *An Illustration of Grace*. She tells the story of her difficulties that faced her in her childhood as a young girl. She then moves on in the story to sharing her years on welfare, being physically abused by the father of her children and then life as a single mother. She understandably could have chosen to remain a victim. Instead she chose to be a creator in her life and tells of how with the emotional support of her family, personal dedication and her spiritual faith she went back to college and earned her law degree. Today she is a successful lawyer in Chicago and her two daughters are a tribute to learning from her example. I liked how she titled her memoir *An Illustration of Grace*. She is a dedicated Catholic and understands how God's grace helped her through her difficulties. This short description does not give her story justice so I recommend you look for her memoir. She is a positive example of resilience in action.

Another story of resilience that does not have such a good ending, yet has powerful memories attached to it is a student I once had in class. His name is Heath. Heath is the one who introduced me to the music of Switchfoot that I use in workshops and several chapters in this book. He had a positive spirit about him and was dedicated to obtaining his welding degree so he could gain a good job to help his single mother and younger brother. That was his dream he told me on the first day of class. One day as he was riding his bike back to his dorm room as a light changed at an intersection and a young driver not paying attention, (to this day the thought is that she was on a cell phone), stepped on the gas and hit Heath on his bike. He flew into the intersection with major head injuries.

When I met his mother at the hospital, Heath was unconscious and paralyzed from the neck down. The medical staff after a week told the mother he was a lost cause and encouraged her to pull the plug on him. Others and I had mentioned to her even though unconscious Heath could still be aware of what was going on and she was encouraged by the prayers so did not follow the doctor's advice. It is good she did not as in a few days his lips started moving and began speaking.

Heath was amazing to visit, as he had such a positive faith about him. He kept telling me, "Sir, I know the Lord is going to allow me to walk again. I want to finish my education and get a job. I don't want to live off the government!". I would leave the room amazed as I knew I could never be that positive if I was in his shoes. Months later he knew he would not walk again but still he was positive. "Sir, I know I won't walk again but my arms work fine! My mom wants her own hair styling shop. I can work the front desk and phones." He always added, "I don't want to live off the government." If only more people had that attitude today. Sad to say he died after his 21st birthday from infection complications. He kept that positive spirit of resilience to the end and he lived to see his mother open up her own hairstyling shop. Heath taught me the importance of keeping a positive resilient spirit. His memory will always be with me as I keep his picture in my office.

At these times when we are knocked down by life that is when our resilience can come into play. Each of our journeys are difference but trouble comes along to each person's journey. The dictionary defines resilience as an ability to recover from or adjust easily to misfortune or change. We can bounce back up from hardships. Dr. Moorer's story, as well as Karla and Heath's stories show we need not need not be completely crushed and debilitated from these events. It is natural to go through the "why me" stage and experience the negative emotions of what we are experiencing. But living a more than ok life means we move beyond the negative feelings to adjust on to a positive pathway.

I want to share one final song from one of my daughter's favorite musicians that I believe relates well to resilience. It is the song "Eye On It" by Toby Mac. The song speaks to some of the techniques that can help people be victors instead of victims in life. The analogy seen in the song is clearly that of a race. Runners are often very resilient, as they understand the need for discipline. They put hours of work and sweat into daily practice of running whether they are sprinters or marathon runners. A runner is not going to win the race or a medal if they spend most of their time lying around surfing the internet and Face booking while constantly snacking on chips and Cola. A runner who lives like that will be lost in a trail of dust. A runner who is serious is disciplined. So to be resilient in life there needs to be an emphasis on living a disciplined life and know what you want out of this life takes work not slacking and snacking.

Then there is the repetition of the phrases in the song "Eye on it" and "Eye on the prize". Resilient people have a focus on their goals. Keeping their eyes set on what they are aiming for. Like a runner they keep pressing forward to their finish line of their goal. Even though they feel the pressure around them and inside of them they do not quit or give up until they cross the finish line. To be a victor you do not give up and quit but keep running the race.

On a grander scale Toby Mac is a Christian musician so I know since I come from the same worldview, the race he is speaking of is that of running the spiritual race of becoming more Christ like. I see in his lyrics a close semblance to the Apostle Paul's writing in:

> I Corinthians 9:24 "Do you not know that in a race all the runners run, but only one gets the prize? Run in such a way as to get the prize."

> Philippians 3:14 "I press on to reach the end of the race and receive the heavenly prize for which God, through Christ Jesus, is calling us."

The Apostle Paul used the race analogy to remind early Christians that this life is about a race of grace in spreading the Good News of Christ while we pass through this quick journey on Earth. So that is the main point Toby Mac is speaking to. Yet from my study and readings on increasing resilience in individuals, the thoughts from the song of—discipline, focus, keeping eyes on the goals relate well to ways to help all people move from being victims of life's problems and hardships to becoming victors.

Reflections:

How is the race you are on this year going? What are you focused on in your life? If you feel like quitting what can you refocus on to keep pressing on?

Think over a past difficulty where you felt overwhelmed. In hindsight can you see how the Hand of God helped through the process whether through other people or in a miraculous happenstance occurrence. Also in these difficult days is there someone you know facing difficulties where you can be the hand of Christ by helping in love?

Do you take the time to use critical thinking in the choices you make?

How do you respond to the external flat tires in your life?

Are there some choices you need to make that may bring new possibilities to your life journey?

Are you a creator or a victim? How can you make wise choices for your life?

Resources for further learning:

D'Souza, Dinesh, Godforsaken, Tyndale, 2012.

Fioni, Karla, An Illustration of Grace, Gabriel Press, 2011.

Glasser, William, Choice Theory, Harper Perrenial, 1999.

Helmstetter, Shad, You Can Excel In Times Of Change, Pocket, 1992.

Mac, Tobey, "Eye On It", Eye On IT—CD.

Moorer, Cleamon, From Failure to Promise, 2010. (check out www. fromfailuretopromise.com)

Reivich, Karen and Shatte, Andrew, The Resilience Factor, Broadway Books, 2002.

Urban, Hal, Life's Greatest Lessons, Touchstone, 2003.

Spiritual Beings In A Material World

I have mentioned that I look at life from a Christian perspective. I believe Spirituality is an important aspect of the Living More Than OK life. This is more a personal point of view not a viewpoint from positive psychology. Yet I am encouraged by Counselor conferences I have gone to recently, I hear a new appreciation for the spiritual aspect of life. Our morals, how we treat others, our purpose in life stems I believe from the spiritual side of life. There are many religious viewpoints, Jewish, Muslim, Hindu. Buddhist, a plethora of other religions and I add atheism in the mix. Actually as I write this I have read articles about an Atheist Church in England that is trying to get branch churches going in the USA. Hearing this I am glad to see there are some honest atheists who are finally admitting that atheism is a belief not a fact like some of the rabid fundamentalist atheists such as Dawkins try to declare. Personally my belief in Christ's death and resurrection in providing a fix to the broken relation with God the Father is an all important driving force in my life. This is the faith that I personally believe. As stated you reading this may follow another point of view which is your right as a free individual.

Matter a fact one of my big pet peeves is when I hear atheists speaking that Christians are people of faith and they atheists are people of science. Hello? Who says Christians are not believers and respecters of science? Look at the history of Science—Johannes Kepler was Lutheran; Robert Boyle was Anglican; Blaise Pascal was a Jansenist; Sir Isaac Newton was Anglican; Louis Pasteur was Catholic; Lord Kelvin William Thompson was Anglican; and you can find many others in today's world and throughout the history of science who believed in God. I do not view Atheism as scientific.

Atheism is a belief as I stated at the beginning. Their belief is that there is no God and it is just that—a belief. Just as they say I as a Christian cannot 100% prove a God exists they cannot prove 100% that no Higher Power or God exists. It is all a matter of faith.

In recent years I have read the works of the new atheists, Christopher Hitchens, Sam Harris, and Richard Dawkins. I am always interested in their arguments against religion. I wanted to compare them with Bertrand Russell's writings as I read his *Why I am Not a Christian?* back when I was searching my doubts on Christianity years ago. I found nothing new in their recent books. I saw just the same extreme hate, misconstruing scriptures out of context and emotional ignorant statements that they state as fact when they are just personal beliefs. The same things they complain about religionists, the hate and emotionalism, they do in their writings but even more exaggerated.

The atheists are most likely more rabid against Christians possibly as Christianity is the dominant faith in the West and in America. What amuses me is how in their writings and atheists I have heard on TV point to those who believe in a religion as following beliefs, (these beliefs are foolish in their viewpoint). On the atheists side they say they promote science so atheism has no aspect of belief. They act like atheism is known fact!. It is to that point I appreciated reading Peter Hitchens' book—*The Rage Against God.* He tells of his journey from atheism back to the Christian faith that He and his atheist brother, (Christopher Hitchens) grew up in. I recommend this book as an insightful spiritual pilgrimage from atheism to Christian faith. In it he so rightly states the atheism just like religious faiths that believe in God are beliefs. All of our world views are based on belief and faith. Ask an atheist what is the scientific proof that proves there is no God? They can't respond as there is no proof that God does not exist. That is what often irks me the most when the atheists speaks of those you believe in a religion hold on to beliefs. Bottom line is the atheist is holding on to a belief with no facts that God does not exist.

Of course I honestly admit I can not prove God exists. I believe it. In Christ we are to live by faith. Although, we are not called, to live an unreasoned faith. I have had my times of doubt in the past and looked at the opposite sides of other religions and atheism and came back thinking Christianity made the most sense to me. My reading years ago of C.S. Lewis's famous book, *Mere Christianity*, made me aware that the Christian faith is a rational faith as it makes sense.

When I was young I remember looking up at the stars and night thinking there has to be something or someone great behind all this. When I have seen the Grand Canyon_or recently visited Niagara Falls_again I look at the majestic beauty and say how can anyone say a God does not exist? Nature seems to shout out like a billboard for God that He is! Appreciating nature won't tell us what kind of God He is. That is where God would need to reveal himself. As a Christian I believe God has revealed Himself through the Bible.

Secular Atheists try to write off religionists and primarily Christians as nuts and fools. The reality is Christianity is a reasoned faith. The Apostle Paul used logical arguments with the Jews and the Greeks to persuade people in his days. Today there are great Christian thinkers like Ravi Zacharias, Josh McDowell, and others who stand up for a rational faith. Ravi Zacharias in his book *The End Of Reason* answers back to Sam Harris' writings. Ravi shares his life story of having his doubts and shows how the emptiness of doubt never fulfilled him as his life in Christ has done.

The hate atheists show towards God is the funniest thing that puzzles me. If they do not believe God exists why are they spewing such hatred towards God? It doesn't make sense. Just state your case and let it be. Reading their God rants I picture in my mind a rabid dog frothing at the mouth barking wildly at a brick wall. What is this non-existent God doing to the poor atheist? Or is it that the true God is speaking to the conscience of the atheist and that is what is setting off their wild rants?

I have heard atheists mention how disappointed Christians will be when they die and they find out nothing exists in the afterlife.

When I read or hear those statements I ponder to myself will I really be disappointed. If the atheist is right will I be disappointed after I die? Will I feel regret that I did not have the pleasure of living a wild life of beer parties falling flat on my face drunk in a pool of vomit? That I missed the pleasure of nearly dying from an overdose of drugs? Or maybe missing the pleasure of sexual freedom with all the accompanying sexually transmitted diseases? Yes those are the true joys of living free without God??

Definitely I will have no regrets. Even if the atheists are right, Christianity has allowed me to live a life of purpose. My faith has given me a basis for living justly and showing kindness to others. It is the basis for living a thankful life for all of the good in life and nature. I can really enjoy life to the full and be happy and better yet with no hangovers! I turn the question around to the atheist. What if they are wrong and they find themselves before the God they told others did not exist? Often in their books from their comfy leather writing chairs they follow Bertrand Russell's argument. They say they would stand firmly before God and politely tell Him he had not given enough evidence to convince them. Yeah right! If God does exist they will not be standing before Him shaking their fist. We won't fully know what is beyond this life, until the curtain falls on this life. The important issue is to understand your belief system and see how it fits with your purposes in life. Does your worldview make sense or are you living a lie? Doubts will come but they help us think through critically what we truly believe.

As a person who believes in the spiritual, sometimes I am faced with the fact that life is not always good. How do I reconcile that with the thought that the Bible shows that God is always good. We all have times when life knocks the air out of us. Moving is not always easy. Trying to adjust to a new job with accompanying stress does not feel good. Finding yourself in a new location without work in the midst of a recession and seeing few job openings but many unemployed competitors does not feel good. On a deeper scale, how do I make sense of the story I state earlier of the student Heath? He was a good Christian student paralyzed by a driver not paying attention and then dying two years later. Or how about a dear friend whose wife died years ago from cancer. Then later his only son dies. Sounds like a modern story of Job. Life is definitely not good at times. It can be downright evil.

Following principles of Positive Psychology that I discuss in this book will not stop the difficulties and travesties of life from appearing in our life journey. Following your personal spiritual faith does not stop these tragedies. As one who follows the Christian worldview I know this to be experientially true. Some falsely assume that a follower of Christ walks down a path strewn with rose petals and angels spreading blessings of happiness, health and wealth in their every moment. That is a false view of Christian reality. Jesus had his share of difficulties and His disciples in the New Testament writings dealt with difficulties and persecutions. They all save, John the Apostle, died cruel deaths. Christian beliefs do not stop evil and difficulties from coming into our lives.

This reality of our life journey brings to mind a Christian song that was popular in the 1990's. It is one of my wife's favorite songs and has an important message for us to reflect on. As usual throughout this book I encourage you to search on YouTube for the song and then reflect over the words of the song, *Life Is Hard But God Is Good* by Pam Thumb.

There is so much emotion of the reality of life in this song. It reminds me of how Scott Peck starts his book The Road Less Traveled—"Life is difficult". It is the hardness and coldness of life that "takes the life out of you . . .". I think of the coldness of what happens in mass killings. People young and old are shot in cold blood by crazed killers begs the question of the silence of where is God in these acts of evil.

The song also, reminds us that the tears of life's pains are not forgotten. There is a Good God behind the difficulties. Even though evil tries to silence God's Grace and Mercy, He will break through the silence if we hold onto hope. God will be faithful to those prayers where you are just kneeling and don't really know what to say as long as you hold on to hope. The difficulties are just a point on our journey they are not the journey itself. At those hardest points in life be assured God silently is walking at your side.

Those who believe in God with the recent emphasis on atheism are made to feel like they are crazy and believing in God is not helpful. The good thing for believers in God is that there are researchers who study the effects of religion and the belief of God in people. The book *How God Changes Your Brain* by Andrew Newberg, M. D. and Mark Waldman shows encouraging research that belief in God can be a positive influence on our lives (as if most Christians and those of other religions don't know this already).

From a neurological standpoint they show primarily how prayer and meditation has health benefits for people. Do they prove God exits? No as they clearly state neurology cannot prove such a thing.

They point out in one area of the book of the mystery of God. I am glad they bring that out in their thinking. As I read the Bible I see there are things that God clearly states and other things he states will remain a mystery. We need to take those unknowns from a mysterious faith standpoint. This reminds me of a quote concerning living the Christian life I heard in a sermon once and wrote down: "To be a witness does not consist in engaging in propaganda or even in stirring people up, but in being a living mystery; it means to live in such a way that one's life would not make sense if God did not exist."—Cardinal Emmanuel Célestin Suhard, Archbishop of Paris 1940–1949—Living as a Christian I should reflect the mystery of God's grace in my actions and speech. Personally, life only makes sense to me as I view it through the lens of a God perspective.

While attending a Keynote speaker session with Dr. Bradford Keeney, at a Counseling conference the importance of the spiritual side of life stood out to me. Dr. Keeney is presently Professor of Marriage and Family Therapy and Hanna Spyker Eminent Scholars Chair in Education, University of Louisiana, Monroe campus. Over the years he has studied healers, shamans, and medicine men around the world in a variety of cultures.

In his presentation Dr. Keeney rightly pointed out that modern Psychology and Counseling relies too much on techniques and theories and neglects what he called the complexity and mystery of the Divine. The sterile secular mindset tries to explain everything and puts everything into categories and stereotypes. He emphasized, Counselors can learn from the ancient healers. Be open to the Spirit. That we gotta have a song in our soul. He brought up the importance of rhapsodic expression of poetry and music. In doing this he went into a beatnik type of rap like poetry expression of his message. I found drawn to his creativeness in his presentation. To help people we do need to tap into creativity and realize that counseling has an art form element to it. The same in all aspects of our life we need to be open to the mystery of the Divine.

A couple of points that made an impression on me was his mentioning of the Irving Mills song, "It Don't Mean A Thing If It Ain't Got That Swing". Dr. Keeney was trying to get across that the healing process is helping people re-energize their lives. Not living an ok existence, but in the liveliness and energy and by the power of the Spirit which is found in his analogy of jazz and spiritual music. Keeping with his music analogy he presented the idea that Counseling needs more song and feeling. Don't just interpret a technique, instead swing and rap with the individual needs, of the person seeking help.

Dr. Keeney at another point began to sing the children spiritual song. "This little light of mine, I'm gonna let it shine." This was a reminder that our purpose in our lives, and in our practice as Counselors is to make the world a brighter place. Life is not about getting things and living complacent ok lives. Instead life is about giving and shining light on the darkness in people's lives. His session impacted my life in a challenging manner of how I can shine my light and be more centered in the spiritual aspect of my life.

Praying along our life journey is an important aspect of the Spiritual life. Understanding the importance of prayer, I slowly and deeply read through a book on Prayer, *A Praying Life: Connecting with God in a Distracting World*, by Paul E. Miller. Paul is the Director of a

Christian ministry SeeJesus which focuses in on interactive Bible Studies and presenting teaching workshops. The title caught my mind as the distractions of the world can pull spiritual minded people away from the importance of prayer.

I purposely read the book in a slow manner as I wanted to think through what he was saying. His book had a completely different feel to it in that he is very open about his prayer life and admits that prayer is a difficult thing to do. He is honest about the cynicism that can come into our prayer life as we see nothing happening so why bother. The author points out that Jesus calls us to a journey of faith and prayer is a big part of that journey. We are encouraged to move beyond our cynicism and pride to embrace our neediness. Paul Miller states "Don't be embarrassed by how needy your heart is and how much it needs to cry out for grace. Just start praying." So the call is to move beyond the distractions and hardships of life and step out in faith.

A couple things that stood out to me is mid way through the book he discusses "Good Asking". He points out in James 4:2-3 the text reads "You do not have because you do not ask." And "You ask and do not receive, because you ask wrongly, to spend it on your passions." These are problems we have with prayer as if we are honest we can complain God is not doing anything in our life but we are not asking for His help. Then on the other hand sometimes our prayers are as selfish as a child rattling off a long list of presents on Santa's lap like God is just our errand boy. We need to strike a balance between not asking or being totally selfish. He sees the answer to both by having a prayer attitude of asking boldly and at the same time surrendering completely to God.

Miller makes a point that, "All of Jesus' teaching on prayer in the Gospels can be summarized with one word: ask. Jesus' greatest concern is that our failure or reluctance to ask keeps us distant from God. God wants to give us good gifts. He loves to give." He backs this up by pointing us to the parables of Jesus about the persistent widow who kept pleading with the judge in the story for help. You can read the whole story in Luke 18:1-8. He also points to the parable of the man bothering a neighbor at night for some bread for his houseguest, see Luke 11:5-8. These thoughts from Jesus point to the fact that just like people will answer persistent asking; how much more will God answer the prayers of His people.

Another thing I enjoyed about the book is his emphasis on the power of story. This is one important aspect I believe about living more than ok is to understand that each of our stories are important. Paul Miller understands that prayer is part of the story. He shows that those who pray with no thought that God is working a story in them are often bitter, angry, aimless, cynical, controlling, hopeless, thankless, blaming. On the other hand those who are open to God's story and seeing His story work through them in their prayer life are waiting, watching, wondering, praying, submitting, hoping, thankful and repenting. This concept of prayer as part of God's story in us relates to near the end of the book the author brings up an idea of a prayer journal or making prayer a part of your journaling. Here are some of his thoughts on prayer journaling, "When life makes sense it becomes a journey, a spiritual adventure. Writing down the adventure as it happens gives us a feel for our place in the story God is weaving in our lives, . . . Many of us rush around without much conscious knowledge of the pilgrimage God is carving out for us. So we slog through life, missing the Divine touches." Life can not be boring and cynical if we are open to seeing God's moments in our lives. To notice these God moments, we need to be living a life of faith and mindfully aware that He is involved in our journey. Prayer is needed in our distracting world that we wake up to every day.

Continuing on the prayer aspect of the spiritual life is a concept of Centering Prayer. I had heard of Centering Prayer in Mindfulness Meditation seminars I had been to. At the same Counselor Conference I mentioned earlier I learned more about Centering Prayer at a Counselor Prayer breakfast I attended. There were not many present that early in the morning, but the presenter shared insight on the importance of prayer that I felt was very timely in my life. She discussed the concept of Centering Prayer. This is meditative and reflective prayer of quietly reflecting for example on a verse from the Bible such as Galatians 5:22 & 23 "But the fruit of the Spirit is love, joy, peace, forbearance, kindness, goodness, faithfulness, gentleness and self-control. Against such things there is no law.". Or you can pray a prayer of worship centered on an attribute of God. She mentioned this moves our prayers away from whiney, gimme, gimme prayers. Not that praying for people and things is wrong but the centered prayer she shared quiets our hearts and calms us to hear from God.

She used the analogy that life with its chaos, fear, sadness, and despair is like a hurricane. Centered prayer allows us to be at peace in the "Eye of the Storm". The eye of the hurricane is where the air is calm and quiet. Having lived in an area that had hurricanes I could appreciate the analogy. As during a hurricane you hear the power of the winds from the first wave of the outer bands. Then all is peaceful in the eye of the storm until the next set of pounding bands of wind hit. Prayer does have that peaceful characteristic to take our spirits away from the rages of the storm to a quiet place in God's presence.

The centering prayer reminds me that listening is often a neglected yet important discipline in the spiritual prayer sphere of our lives. In the American Christian tradition which is the basis of my worldview, prayer is too often a one sided gabfest with God. With our ongoing list and repetition of demands and requests to the Almighty, there is no silence and listening on our part. If we look at prayer and meditation as communing with God there must be listening on our part.

These two following verses from the Psalms remind us of the importance of listening to God with our inner spirit waiting silently in His presence.

Psalm 85:8 "I will listen to what God the LORD says he promises peace to his people, his faithful servants—but let them not turn to folly."

Psalm 62:5 "For God Alone, O my soul waits in silence, for my hope is from Him." If we seriously want peace and to live in the hope God provides, we need to be listening for His call in our lives. To be considered as faithful servants as the Psalmist says, we need to be listeners to God the Fathers voice. I take note of the word folly in the first verse mentioned. Often in going our own way because we are not listening to God, we fall into folly and foolishness in our actions and face the negative consequences.

A dear friend of mine from Chicago singer/songwriter, Keryn Moriyah has an original song she wrote entitled *Listen*. View the lyrics and reflect how they relate to prayer and especially the concept of centering prayer. You can also find the video of her song on YouTube.

> Listen by Keryn Moriyah
>
> Look at the world in a rumble. See the people tremblin", tremblin".
>
> Refrain:
>
> Listen. Can you hear me? Listen, you should be listening to my call.
>
> Sensitivity is scarce, touching is rare. Caring is becoming extinct and
>
> loving is on the brink, so . . .
>
> Refrain Walk in new life in the Spirit, for He is strong and we are weak,
>
> so weak, so weak to worship the Father and love one another.
>
> Yeshua, Covenant of the redeemed!

Ending Refrain: Listen, can you hear me? Listen, can you hear me? Hear me.

Listen, can you hear me, hear me? Listen, you should be listening to my call.

Listen, (to my Lord's call) can you hear me?(. . . to my Lord's call). Listen.

I will never forget you . . . never forsake you listen, listen, listen, listen, listen.

The song to me is a prophetic call to us in troubled times to take time to listen to the Lord God's voice. When we are feeling forgotten and forsaken we are reminded by the song that God does not forget us. He can be our strength when we are overcome by the folly and foolishness in the world that causes us to tremble. When we do not take time to listen we become overburdened and downtrodden so that we cannot care and love as we should.

If we take time to be quiet and listen and understand that this is part of worshipping God, we can enjoy the covenant relationship with the Lord. He will then guide us in seeing the needs around us that He wants us to reach out to. He will give us His strength to love the world that is in a rumble of trouble. Following this way is true walking in the Spirit.

The thought that we are spiritual being in a material world affects should ideally affect the way we live our lives. Just as the quote I mentioned by Cardinal Emmanuel Célestin Suhard our lives need to reflect and show the mystery of God's grace and mercy. One of the best songs that relate to living the spiritual life from the Christian worldview is the Peace Prayer of St. Francis of Assisi that was adapted for song my Catholic Monk John Michael Talbot. I have the words listed here as this prayer encapsulates much of what the Christian life is about I believe.

Peace Prayer, By St. Francis of Assisi adapted by John Michael Talbot

Lord, make me an instrument of Your peace.
Where there is hatred, let me sow love
Where there is injury, pardon.
And where there is doubting let me bring Your faith.
And Lord, make me an instrument of Your peace.
Where there is despairing, let me bring Your hope.
Where there is darkness, Your light.
And where there is sadness, let me bring Your joy.
Oh Divine Master, grant that I might see,
not so much to be consoled as to console.
To be understood as to understand
Not so much to be loved as to love another.
For it is in giving that we now receive
it is in pardoning that we are now pardoned
and it is in dying that we are now born again
And Lord, make me an instrument of Your peace.
Where there is hatred let me bring Your love

Whether in our work life, family life, or recreational life we who say we follow the way of Christ, need to have the mindset that we are instruments in the hands of God to show the world His peace, hope and love. We need to be consoling to those who are hurting and joyful to those who need cheered up. To a doubting world we need to show true faith. St Francis showed in his words that it is nothing Christians can do in their own power it is through the humility of allowing God's Spirit to work through us as instruments of peace. If Christians truly lived this way the negative sterotypes would mostly fall away.

Living out the St Francis prayer, addresses a wrong viewpoint about Christians and Christianity. It speaks to the thought that Christians just sit around in their churches waiting to die so they can really live in heaven. Granted there are some Christians that are so heavenly minded they are no earthly good. Sad to say I have met people who cannot stand Christianity because they have run ins with Christians like those. That is one point where I sometimes understand where the atheists are coming from. They only see Christians as mad and sad. That is not how God intends Christians to live.

Christians that create these ideas that this life is all sorrow and sadness until we reach heaven are painting a false picture that the writer of a song by the band Switchfoot reacts to. We forget that Jesus was accused of carousing with sinners and gluttons. His first miracle was at a wedding. The disciples would try to chase children away from Him and Jesus would chide them as He enjoyed paying attention to children. As I have stated before, Jesus stated He came to give us life and life abundantly. Jesus wanted His followers to live in the present fully as well as look forward to the future finalized Kingdom.

Check out the song *Afterlife,* by Switchfoot by listening to the video of it online on the internet. The song starts out with a spiritual thought of tasting fire which makes me think of the Story in The Book at Acts of the tongues of fire which was a testimony of the Holy Spirit of God in the early Christian believers. In Christians are to come alive as energized like a fire. The song then moves into an analogy of the sunshine burning his skin; heating him up. I don't know about you but after a few grey cloudy days I always feel more alive when the rays of sunshine break through and warm me up.

His phrase, "I still believe we could live forever", and the name of the song shows he believes in an afterlife. Heaven that is beyond our imagination in splendor, is a reality I believe in, and the songwriter shows he believes it. I appreciate how he says, "You and I we begin forever now". The spiritual relationship with God begins not when we die but now. We are not to sit on the sidelines through our time here, but to be active participants in enjoying the journey God has for us for our time on this planet.

I think of how in C. S. Lewis' writings he portrayed the fleeting nature of this life as a proof of sorts, for the afterlife. This life goes by so quickly there has to be something more out there. This life is a foreshadow of what is to come in a more splendorous fashion. Sure there are many difficulties in this life and we each experience those times. Yet are we made to dwell on those and miss out on good times with family and friends, or appreciating the simple beauty of Spring flowers. "Everyday A choice is made Everyday I choose my fate". Each day we can wake up and choose to dwell on the negative pains of life or choose to catch the Spirit's fire and fully enjoy what God has waiting for us each day. A saying of C.S. Lewis states: "Aim at heaven and you will get earth thrown in. Aim at earth and you get neither" This puts the song lyrics in perspective. We do not want to have tunnel vision on just looking at life on this earth. Focusing on this life only will drag a person down. In keeping a forever focus we can look forward with anticipation to the promise of heaven. Also we can enjoy the full joy of living in our present life as well.

A help in our spiritual being can be to look at for Spiritual heroes. Each spiritual tradition has their own spiritual figures to look up to. From what I gather about the new atheist churches they look to great past atheists as their heroes. Since I am writing from the Christian standpoint of course I turn to the Christian scriptures. Looking to heroes to respect and learn from is important in improving our lives. In the beginning of each semester in the College Success courses I teach I ask the students a question, "Who is a hero that you look up to?". Some students look quizzically at me so I explain further what I mean. Who do they admire and respect to the point that they would like to be like that person? Often the response is a family member or relative. Some mention historical figures or religious figures. Every now and then a comic book hero comes up like Superman or Spiderman. It is an important question as it is helpful as to how we shape our lives. Often a significant person has an effect on how we shape our lives. As we view people or read stories of people of high ethical character, courage, and creativity their stories and life examples can encourage us to improve how we live our lives.

The importance of heroes from a spiritual standpoint struck me by reading the book—*The Heroes of Faithfulness* by Steve Barckholtz. He is a former Pastor who has followed a career path that he feels God has called him to as a fulltime writer. His book is an in-depth look at Hebrews chapter 11. Over the years I have heard many sermons on Sundays about Hebrews 11. Often the messages call the chapter the Bible's Hall of Fame of heroes. The chapter is a listing of many of the famous Biblical cast of characters: Noah, Abraham, Jacob, Joseph, Moses, Samson, David and many others that people often look up to from the Old Testament. Is this chapter simply about hero worship of these people?

Steve in his book offers a twist on the often considered thought that this is a chapter concerning the heroes of the faith that we should look up to. He takes the reader through a personal look at each of these biblical characters showing their human failings. He reminds us that they are people just like us not to be worshipped. He then shows though, how God had a unique plan for each of them that was developed not by their own greatness but by their faith in a Faithful God. The book opens the reader's eyes to the real hero of the chapter. The hero we should be following is Jesus Christ. He is the faithful one who will not disappoint and faithfully be there in our time of need.

Steve Barckholtz, by reminding us to keep our hero eyes on Jesus, Christians can trust Jesus to work out God's plan for each of those who believe in him. The stories that we are reminded of in Hebrews 11 are of people who followed the faithfulness of God with a deep faith and accomplished amazing things for God. Moses a man on the run for murdering an Egyptian became the man who led Israel out of bondage. David started out as a shepherd and youngest of his family but became the great King of Israel. One of my favorites, the story of Joseph who endured abuse and injustice throughout much of his life, was one who would have had every reason to turn his back on God with a chip on his shoulder. Instead Joseph kept his faith in God and was lifted up to a position to preserve Egypt and God's people Israel during a great time of famine.

I was struck by Steve's description for the type of faith God desires in our lives. He taps into Jesus' parable of the Mustard seed in Matthew 13. He reminds the reader what Jesus was getting at, was not to simply stay with faith the size of a small seed but the listener in those times would understand the mustard seed would grow as he describes it, "an outrageously large, wild and unkempt tree." (page 225). He goes on to say the God does not want us to live with minimal just getting by faith but a faith that is "large, crazy, wild and out of control". Meaning—out of our control but living in God's faithful control. It is a faith that helps in living out God's plan for our lives. That is a very challenging thought on how to live our life but it fits well my thinking which has been the basis for my blog— Living More Than OK.

In closing this chapter did I disprove atheism and prove that the Christian God is the true God? No, as I stated earlier all Beliefs: Judaism, Islam, Christianity, Buddhism, Atheism, and every other "ism" are based on our faith not science. Yet for me I believe 100% that Christianity makes sense for me. Some Christians may not like me saying it this way, but a clear reading of the Bible shows that we turn to the work of Jesus on the cross and raised the third day by faith not rational arguing. Yet one proof for every true Christian is God's Spirit living inside and empowering Christians to live love boldly in the world. This I see in a song, God's Not Dead (Roarin Like A Lion) The Newsboys. There are many videos of this song on the internet.

Their song is a bold proclamation of their faith in a living God. Hope arises through this faith that we have in the risen Christ. Their proclamation reminds me of the verse, Romans 1:16 "For I am not ashamed of the gospel, because it is the power of God that brings salvation to everyone who believes: first to the Jew, then to the Gentile." In a world where atheists label believers as crazy we can stand and boldly respond to their secular religious faith in "No God". The verse says, "it is the power of God that brings salvation to everyone who believes." Yes it all boils down to belief. But as we read through the Pauline epistles we understand it is a belief based upon sound reasonable arguments. Just because I can't place God in a test tube or beaker does not mean He ceases to exist.

God's clear existence is seen in the lyrics, "He's roarin like a lion". The lion is a symbol of God. In Revelation 5:5 Jesus the Messiah is pictured as the Lion of the tribe of Judah. The atheist declares where is God? Why is he silent? Is the lion's roar silent? I hear the Lion's roar of God when I've seen the Grand Canyon, looking out at the waves of the Pacific Ocean, or seeing the changed lives of people. Going back to the Easter story, look at the changed lives of the disciples. There is no rational explanation other than the resurrection of Jesus that the cowering, fearful disciples should have turned around with most of them giving up their lives for the message of the gospel. Think about it.

One other thought, hearing of the Roar of the Lion, for me is seen at the beginning of the song. That is seeing Christ's love work through His people. "Let love explode And bring the dead to life A love so bold To see a revolution somehow Let love explode And bring the dead to life". John 13:35 states, "By this all men will know that you are my disciples, if you love one another". If Christians would live out that love that would be a pretty loud roar! Sad to say many don't.

Again I can only look at the aspect of Spirituality from my worldview which is as a Christian. If you are reading this and not of that belief system I hope this at least help you see a little of where we Christians are coming from in our beliefs.

Reflection:

Reflect over who is a hero in your life? What Bible character have you especially connected with in your reading of the Bible? What does it mean to you to have God as your hero? What does it mean to have a large wild and crazy faith?

In your personal prayer and/or meditation time are you taking time to quietly listen to God's speaking to you? Incorporate time of listening in your spiritual devotional prayer time.

Take some time to think through your belief system your worldview. Try to draw a picture of it or write a poem about it. How do your beliefs affect your purpose and happiness in life? If you are curious about what this Christian thing and Christ is all about—try reading through the book of Mark or John in the Bible. As you read through reflect over who Jesus is and who he said he is?

Think back to a difficulty in your life journey. From your vantage point now, can you see what you learned from the experience that can help you in further difficult times? Take a moment to breathe a prayer for those around the world in major difficulties.

How are you shining your light in your world to make it a better place? Do you have an inner song that inspires your life?

Where are you at in your prayer life with the balance between asking boldly and being submissive to God's will in your life? Take some time to journal about the concept of prayer being part of God's story in your life.

Resources for further learning:

Barckholtz, Steve, The Heroes of Faithfulness, Xulon, 2013.

Hitchens, Peter, The Rage Against God, Zondervan, 2011.

Lewis, C.S., Mere Christianity, Harper, 2009.

Miller, Paul, A Praying Life: Connecting with God in a Distracting World, Nav Press, 2009.

Newberg, Andrew & Waldman, Mark, How God Changes Your Brain, Ballantine, 2009.

Follow Your Purpose With Passion

During one of my recent nuclear stress tests for my heart, the instructions had a suggestion to bring something to read as the whole process takes several hours. Much of that time is waiting between pictures of the heart at rest and after being on the treadmill. So I noticed in my books to read pile was a small book, *Noble Purpose: The Joy of Living a Meaningful Life* by Dr. William Damon. I felt I could finish it during the waiting times so I took it to the Heart Clinic.

This book is a short book as I finished it during my time in the waiting room during the 3 ½ hours. Even though it was short, the impact of the message was very big in my thoughts. This is one of those books where I feel the world would be a better place if everyone would read it. I truly believe we are created as purpose driven. God has a purpose for each of us. So connecting our interests and God given strengths helps us to discover our career and non-career purposes in life.

The core thought of his book is found in these statements by the author, "A life built around noble purpose is a life well spent . . . . Commitment to a noble purpose, apart from the good that it produces for the world, endows a person with joy in good times and resilience in hard times." (pgs. 66–67). That is what Living More Than OK is all about. In living a more than OK life we need to be following greater purposes for our lives. What causes are important to you? How does the life you live impact your family and friends for the better?

That word "noble" in the title, I had never thought of before in relation to purpose in life. The author made me realize that we need to reflect over our purposes. My purpose does not have to be at the level of a hero or famous person. The key is—are my purposes moral? Is my purpose just for selfishness of acquiring as much stuff I can store in my house or at a storage center? Is my purpose just about money? God centered purposes focus outward from the self to touch others' lives for the better.

Near the end of the book, Dr. Damon presents 9 principles to help in our building a purpose filled life. I will paraphrase them here. First of all is to start with a purpose. Find an interest or cause you are passionate about and become involved. If you are having difficulty finding a purpose look at the close areas of your life as in your family, your church, social organizations, your career. Wherever you find most of your energy expended is a good place to find a purpose. Next, look for purpose driven examples in others that you can follow. These may be found in a mentor at your workplace or maybe a historical figure you have read about. Another good idea is to look for support from others. Share your purpose with others and see if anyone wants to join you. Or maybe your purpose in found in your religious faith so check in your local congregation to see if you can find others to join you. With following your purpose be wary of perfectionism. There are always bumps along the way to discourage you. Don't let discouragement defeat your purpose God has given you.

If you are counting—the next is his sixth principle of keeping a humble heart in following your purpose. This fits well with his concept of noble purpose. To keep our spiritual compass on a moral plane, we need to keep our pride in check with humility. Along with humility then keep a focus on keeping your purpose noble by reviewing the means you are using to reach the goal of your purpose. This is counter culture in a world where the emphasis is use any means even immoral means of lying and cheating to gain your advantage. Staying noble is looking at the morality of your purpose journey from point A to point B. Number 8 is have a thankful heart of celebration for the purpose you are seeking to achieve. This allows for joy in the journey in what you are trying to accomplish in your career or other aspects of your life. Then the last principle is similar to point three, you should look for examples to follow. Principle 9 is be an example yourself to others. Disciple others, mentor others, especially younger people, in living a purpose driven life so others can have ". . . a life well spent".

There is much more than these 9 principles packed into this little powerful book. I again highly recommend it. But more importantly take time to look at your purposes for living your life journey.

One way to help keep a focus on your purpose in life is to develop and compose a Personal Mission Statement. The Personal Mission Statement zeroes in on your core values, principles, and key items you wish to accomplish with your life. In Stephen Covey's book The 7 Habits of Highly Effective People he likens the Mission Statement to that of the Unites States Constitution, the core values of our country.

Before working on the Mission Statement there is a need to work on concepts that go into it. Take time to brainstorm a list of values that are important to you. What are some of the positive strong qualities that set you apart from the next person? Make a list of 10 of the most important things in your life. Think over and list 5 core principles that are unchangeable and are the basis for your worldview and lifestyle.

Just as the Constitution is the standard for our country the Personal Mission Statement is the standard to guide our sense of purpose through the storms of life. Our world is always changing but a mission statement can help remind us of the inner strengths and principles we believe in that do not change. It can help us keep moving towards our goals and pursuits in our life journey by providing a guideline to keep on track with what is important to us.

The Mission Statement also helps us be more responsible so more can be accomplished of what we really want for our lives. Stephen Covey quotes the Psychiatrist Victor Frankel in his section on Mission statements. "Ultimately, man should not ask what the meaning of his life is, but rather must recognize that it is he who is asked. In a word, each man is questioned by life; and he can only answer to life by answering for his own life; to life he can only respond by being responsible." We are responsible for our choices and following our personal beliefs. Understanding our responsibility to follow our mission statement encourages a deeper motivation and commitment to live our daily life by the principles and values important and keep a vision towards being goal centered which is important in living more than ok.

Keep your Mission Statement in a place you can review it often. Place it at your desk, as a wall poster hanging in your office or bedroom, or laminate a small version to place in your wallet or purse. This way you can review it on a regular basis and keep in fresh in your mind as a guiding force in your life. Does the Mission Statement ever change? As we go through shifts in our lives aspects of our life change but our core principles are usually constant unless a major philosophical and spiritual shift occurs. As we review our Mission Statements during periods of shifts there are new items that may need added and others replaced.

Here is a rough draft to my Personal Mission Statement:

- I seek to live a life pleasing to God as I follow the principles of Christ like living to the best of my ability.

- I seek to be a positive loving support to my wife and daughter in the journey God has for them.

- I am committed to grow in my creative and critical thinking skills in helping others grow to reach their God given potential of living more than OK.

- I desire to live a more simple life to appreciate the savoring of God moments in life.

- I desire to live a thankful life for all that God brings into my life journey.

Get on Mission in your life. Take time to work on your Personal Mission Statement. Start by listing your core principles, values, things and people that are important to you. You can then write it out in a poem format, listing of declarative statements or in a narrative form. If you are really creative maybe do a poster using drawing along with your statements. If you have difficulty in thinking on how to do a mission statement simply go on the internet to your favorite search engine and simply search "Personal Mission Statements" and you will find examples.

Metaphors are a helpful way to think through aspects of our lives such as purpose and where to direct our life passion. A book that makes the use of metaphors in relation to life direction that has impacted my thinking on purpose is *A Tale Of Three Ships* by Dwight Edwards. He is an author, Pastor of a church in Houston and President of High Octane for the Mind. The book is a great gift item for a high school or college graduate as it can help them shape their life direction in relation to their purpose in life. Dwight looks at our lives as being in one of three stages and to describe the stages he uses the metaphors of ships.

His driving thrust is that we are created for a purpose. To go beyond just existing in life or just getting by, or where we look back and see that life has past us by in our final days we need passion and purpose. In that search in our life we are on at one time or another one of three ships. It is our choice which one we spend the most time on.

The first one he writes of is the Sinking Ship. Doesn't sound like a nice one, but in reality look around at the people you see, look around at the news on TV or the internet. You find that too many people spend much of their life time on that ship. This is the ship where we are living in survival mode. "Most men lead lives of quiet desperation and go to the grave with the song still in them."— Henry David Thoreau. This quote describes this ship rather well. There is a song in each of us that is meant to be shared with the world. For most sadly it remains silent as they allow life to pass them buy just like a herd of cows grazing and sleeping life away.

Never trying anything new or taking a risk. Just living paycheck to paycheck and waiting for life to end.

The second ship is the cruise ship. Now we are talking. If you have never taken a cruise you should try it. All your comforts are met, food anytime you desire, and totally relaxing. The cruise ship is a metaphor for a life full of materialism and the pursuit of the pleasure principle. Is life just about acquiring more stuff than the next person? Living just for pleasure and material things leaves us in the end with just a bunch of stuff at the end of life. King Solomon's one major theme in the book of Ecclesiastes in the Bible is that a life striving after things is just vanity. This again does not mean it is wrong to enjoy a vacation, a movie night, a fine restaurant, ect. The question is should that be a focal point of our existence? Ponder over these words by psychologist, William James, "The greatest use of life is to spend it for something that will outlast it." He was speaking of doing significant things in our life. Our toys and material stuff just wind up in resale shops or junk yards after our death.

The final ship is the battleship. This is not about starting fights, the author is using the battleship as a metaphor for making a difference or having a significant impact in life. This hearkens back to the previous William James quote. This ship looks at a life where having a significance and a purpose in your life is an important focal point. The author terms it as having a noble cause. Here he quotes one of my favorite authors Psychiatrist Victor Frankl, "Everyone has his own specific vocation or mission in life; everyone must carry out a concrete assignment that demands fulfillment. Therein he cannot be replaced, nor can his life be repeated, thus, everyone's task is unique as his specific opportunity." Frankl's words take us back to the concept that we all have a purpose for our life. Part of the adventure is finding the purpose and living it out.

As I look back most of my life has been mostly on the sinking ship and a journey on the battleship with a little bit of cruise ship tossed in. The author points out that we spend time on each ship. In seeking the best life possible and living an exceptional life we need to focus in on ship number three the battle ship—living for a noble cause.

In Counseling there is a technique called cinematherapy. This is using movie clips or whole movies in the therapeutic healing process. Instead of saying 'Take one aspirin and call me in the morning" it is more like "Take one Walt Disney and call me in the morning." Even though I am a licensed Counselor I admit I was skeptical when I first heard of cinematherapy. Then after hearing of this technique in a lecture the next time I saw a movie in the theater, I caught myself paying attention to the plot and the characters in a deeper way. I then felt there is a point that we can learn from the stories we see in the movies. On this topic of living with passion and purpose a movie, 7 *Days in Utopia* came into my mind. I am not a golfers so, I had put off seeing it thinking it just a golf movie. As I finally saw the movie I watched the story unfold. I saw several life principles at work. One primary one was for the young lead character to learn life was more than golf. The movie presents principles that can be transferred into any person's career life and personal life balance.

The opening of the movie has Luke Chisholm exploding in anger over a disintegrating performance in a golf game. As he is recklessly driving due to his emotions he crashes through a rancher's fence. The elderly rancher, John, comes to his rescue and requests he stay with him for 7 days to get his golf game back. There are many dynamics in the story. Does Luke really want to play golf? Or was that his dad's dream for him? There is shown in flash backs the tensions between he and his father, who was his over demanding coach and caddy. This made me wonder if golf was really Luke's thing or his dad's. I have seen that working with college students where they feel their parents are pushing them in one direction that differs to what they really desire.

Instead of just playing golf John, who was a former golfer himself, has Luke do other things that relate to golf but initially seem very strange. Just one for an example, he has him study a golf shot in a wooded area and the instead of just hitting the ball has him paint the view of hitting the ball first. So the idea was to tap into creativity and that particular example was encouraging a deep level of visualizing before trying the difficult shot. John is trying to get Luke to explore his passion level for golf and to allow him to see God has a purpose for his life greater than golf. Life is more than just a job or career we need to discover our greater purpose.

I was impressed by the concept of SFT, (See, Feel, Trust) that comes up in the movie early as John is speaking about Luke's putting. John emphasizes that Luke should not think but to See, Feel, and Trust. There is a truth in that, that we in our work have to move beyond over thinking to See, which means to visualize the big picture of what you are doing, Then Feel is having confidence in the visualization process to move forward. Finally to trust is to step out and act on that confidence to complete what you are trying to do. As I watched that work out in the film; the SFT concept reminded me of Psychologist, Dr. Cziksentmihalyi's Flow concept, of having a sense of mastery and trust in your competence so that you are not over thinking but you are one with your work that you are doing.

The movie goes deeper into the SFT concept looking at it in a spiritual level. John tells Luke near the end of the movie to make Luke understand that he needs to find a greater purpose in life than golf. How does Luke want to be remembered after his life is over? Here John explains that he needs to See God's face, Feel God's presence and Trust God's love—SFT. Looking at life from a God centered perspective, it was no accident that Luke turned towards Utopia. Granted, he could have taken the other turn and gone to another town and not experienced the 7 days in Utopia. But God had a purpose for Luke to be there. In those 7 days, he had the opportunity to understand that relationships are important, reflect on his passion and conviction level for golf and reach a point of feeling the presence of God. As I believe we are spiritual beings, I feel we need to first know who God is by seeing His face and feeling His presence. Then we can learn to trust in His love and know as is stated in Jeremiah 29:11 "For I know the plans I have for you," declares the LORD, "plans to prosper you and not to harm you, plans to give you hope and a future." God has good plans for us even after a terrible game or problem occurs. That is a truth and promise we can hold onto in difficult and good times.

That choice to make the turn to Utopia reminds me as well, to Dr. John Krumboltz's concepts on Happenstance in creating our own luck. Luke did not plan the accident. It happened. Yet there were a multitude of choices he could have made about the situation and then there were the choices he did make. We can't change the bad things that happens. We cannot change the chaos of life. What we do have control over is the choices we make after the fact.

At this point in the movie the older ex golf pro gives Luke a box. In it is a Bible, a note from John, a pencil and two pieces of paper. With the papers Luke is told to draw up two lists. One is a list of all the lies he has listened to about himself. For Luke lies such as his self-worth is based in how well he does with a little white golf ball. Lies that he told himself such as his father only cared about him if he did well in golf. We each over our lifetime can fill our minds with lies about ourselves which can spiral us down in to subpar just ok existing instead of the abundant life we were created for. That list of lies he was to write was to be buried in the box as a symbol of being rid of the lies. The other sheet of paper Luke was to write down truths about himself that he was to keep as a remembrance to give him strength in his life going forward. What are truths we can write and hold onto? Truths such as God loves us, and has a greater purpose for our lives. That we each have talents, that we each have unique inner strengths that can be used to help improve the lives of those around us. We need to focus on the truths and not the lies.

If you have not seen this movie I highly recommend it. Enjoy the story and acting. Then also think through your life as to how the See, Feel, Trust concept relates to your life. Think through the greater purpose there is for you in your living more than ok on your life journey.

One of my favorite positive psychology principles is the concept of Flow that was brought to popularity years ago by Dr. Mihalyi Csikszentmihalyi, a professor of Positive Psychology and Creativity now at Claremont Graduate University. I believe it is one of the key concepts in overcoming the boredom in life which is part of Living More than OK. As we can move to more than OK, by becoming aware of Flow moments and activities in our lives. This is a vital aid in building our level of purpose in life and in increasing our passion for living.

Flow is that experience where you are totally absorbed in what you are doing? It occurs most often when we are doing things we enjoy. One definition of it is, "The state of complete absorption and interest in a task occurring when ability/skill and challenge are high". Have you ever been involved in a favorite activity and it felt like time stopped and you were able to accomplish more than you imagined you could? You were in a Flow state. Much of Dr. Csikszentmihalyi's research initially was on sports and musicians—studying their flow states as Flow in seen easily in these activities.

One may think if Flow just happens why study it? I appreciated in Dr. Csikszentmihalyi's books how in his research of the issue his main concern is for people to live living happier and more complete lives. People living more fulfilling lives and moving beyond the mundaneness of boredom is one main reason I started my blog and created my desire to write a book to help people improve their lives. If being aware of Flow helps people live more fulfilled then a thought that comes to my mind is how can we increase the amount of time we are experiencing flow? Of course we can't live in complete absorption all of the time. Dr Csikszenmihalyi points out that we can't be in flow all of the time. If we were we would be like a world of Energizer Bunnies or Flow itself would become boring.

Flow is often found in the activities you really enjoy doing. Next time you are doing your favorite activity, photography, writing, fishing, quilting, or gardening see afterwards if you felt re-energized by the activity. Ask yourself what activities do you do where you feel like time just flies by. Did you feel a deeper sense of concentration? Most likely you were in Flow.

In the studies on Flow, there were common aspects of those who experienced flow. Here are some of the main aspects. One is having Goals. Clear specific concrete goals can help us improve in our lives and enhance our opportunities of flow experiences. The goals are guides often for the activities we enjoy doing and desire to excel in them. Again the example of sports comes to mind. Coaches and athletes often make use of goals in their practice and competition.

Concentration and focus are helpful in attaining flow. I have observed artists at their canvas and they don't distractingly look around but are absorbed in their work on the canvas. If you watch Sport stars in gymnastics and ice skating you can see intensity in their eyes as they are mentally focusing at the task at hand. Some sports stars will mention in interviews that they are often visualizing their performance in their split seconds before the game or sports activity. We have great power given to us to focus on our tasks if we tap into that power God has given us in our minds.

Importance of having a balance of ability and challenge is another aid to flow. Dr. Mihalyi Csikszentmihalyi in his research looked at ability levels. Flow occurs when we feel challenged yet we have enough knowledge and ability to have confidence in that we can meet the challenge. If we don't have the ability to do the activity then frustration occurs which is definitely not a flow experience. We can continue to improve as we grow in our abilities to reach higher levels of expertise on those things we enjoy doing.

Another main aspect I would like to point out is then merging our awareness and action together. With the goals and focus in place we then move into doing the activity. Here we do the activity and we simply enjoy doing it. Mental activity and physical action merge into oneness as we paint, swim, jog, write or sew. Now flow occurs and we don't overanalyze. What stops the flow is if we start to judge ourselves—"what are others thinking of me?" "Am I doing this right?" Leave the questions for a later reflection time simply do it! For example a swimmer in a race doesn't have the opportunity mid-race to stop and reflect on his progress. Reflection on performance has its place after the activity but to win the race the swimmer must stay in the flow of the race experience trusting his talents.

By making use of flow activities in our lives we can enjoy our daily life more. It guides us to learn the areas in life where we have more passion about so we can live more passionately. We can continue to improve and find delight is our favorite activities. Also since focus and concentration are part of the Flow experience we can build up our ability to focus better in other activities by replicating the power of focus in our flow activity. Another benefit to flow is that we are exercising our mind so our mental facilities are strengthened. As we increase our ability level our ability to reach new challenges grows. This can aid in improvement in creativity as we consider new ways to engage in our favorite activities. The more we make use of flow in life the more we have opportunities to enjoy the life journey we are on with passion.

What is it that shapes our outlook on each day and our future? How can several people experience the same event and have totally different feelings and ideas about it? One person looks at a rainy day as a terrible nuisance and another thinks it is helpful for the plants and nature or enjoys it as a great day to relax and read, (my personal favorite). This shaper of our mental outlook is our attitude. Our attitude corresponds to our level of passion for life and living. We all have an attitude all the time. The problem is what kind of attitude do we carry around with us?

There is a motivational company called Simple Truths that promotes positive books on a variety of topics. They also have short motivational videos that are very uplifting to the spirit and can help think over better ways to live our lives. One of my favorites of their books is *Attitude Is Important*. There are too many uplifting ideas in this book to expound on in this short chapter. I just want to touch on a few that meant the most to me as I watched it. The first is what I think most of us relate to when considering attitude. Stay Positive. A positive attitude is so important to living the best life possible. I often ask college students in lecture who would you rather hang around with? Someone with a positive attitude towards life or a negative attitude? Always the response is the desire to be with a positive attitude person. There is always the rare wise aleck student that states they enjoy negativity.

To have the best life possible and live with a sense of purpose, we need to have an attitude that "Expects the Best". If we expect the best, that attitude motivates us to do our best to get what we desire. To go for our dreams and reach our goals we need to have that expectation of the best to fully reach them. Listen to testimonials of sport stars and musicians you will often catch that "expecting the best attitude" in their talk. This drives their discipline to be the best. We each can use that attitude in achieving what we each are passionate about.

Attitudes are relational as they affect how we relate to those around us. The thought in the book about an attitude of kindness is important to consider. "It is not the things you get, but the hearts you touch that will determine your success in life". The kindness attitude seeks to help build other people up not to tear them down. A good question to ask in relating to others is how do we view others? Is it with a kind heart or a disdainful heart? Greater than kindness, is having a loving attitude. The quote from the book is so true which I believe is why they call their company Simple Truths. "Love doesn't make the world go round—Love is what makes the ride worthwhile." To live a life of purpose and fulfill our mission God has us in this life for is to be people with loving attitudes. This is why the Bible states the "greatest of these is love" in I Corinthians 13.

Another question I found important in this book on attitude speaks of how attitudes are contagious. Attitudes can rub off on others. Consider a work situation where negative comments are being tossed about by a worker who has a bad attitude. Soon others chime in and try to one up the negative statements. The work climate soon becomes very negative and gloomy. Consider the same work group situation but this time a positive attitude person encourages a co-worker and is always cheerful and kind. Often then the office atmosphere becomes more positive. So here is an important question to consider—Is my attitude worth catching?

Often our passion and purpose in life are bathed in difficulties and failures we face in life. I want to look deeper at one character I mentioned in the chapter on resilience as his was and still is a life of purpose. It is the story of Dr. C. Moorer from his book, *From Failure To Promise: An Uncommon Path To Professoriate*. As I stated Dr. C. Moorer is a business professor now at a school in Detroit so he has come full circle in his life back to his hometown. He also is President of Dr. C. Moorer & Associates. It is an organizational foundation that is guided by the thoughts behind this quote—"Life's most persistent and urgent question is, 'What are you doing for others?'" Dr. Martin Luther King, Jr. They offer students and educators scholarships and work on issues related to global poverty.

I share Dr. Moorer's story with my college students as it is a story of a young man with dreams of success interrupted by failure. Sad to say over the years I have seen failure derail college students from reaching their dreams and defeating their purpose for their lives. Some of them just give up and that mentality is the basis for much of the statistics concerning people who do not finish their college education. There are not too many people who move from high school to college and then on to business success without any periods of failure in their lives. All of us experience failure at some level. The key is what do we do when we fail? Do we just give up and spiral down into more difficulties or do we rise up and move forward?

Dr. Moorer shares how after high school he left for Engineering School with a dream to be an engineer. His background was that of a good Christian home with supportive parents. Educationally he went to a Magnet School in Detroit and he admits it was in a poor crime ridden area. In the story though the reader understands he had a strong Christian faith that bolstered him and that gratefully came from sincere Christian parents.

He had the passion for engineering and was even given an opportunity to intern at an auto company. Yet he states that he flunked out of GMI Engineering Institute after being placed on suspension. I have been on Suspension committees at Universities I have worked at in the past, so I know what he went through. He honestly shares what I have observed in a number of students over the time I have worked at colleges and a university. His public school education had not adequately prepared him for the rigors of an engineering education. There were concerns of his parent's health as well that weighed on his mind during the semesters that added stress. There is also a statement in the text as he was going into his finals exams picturing well his fear of failure which is often a self-fulfilling prophecy no matter how hard the student studies in the end.

What was refreshing about his story is he is honest instead of trying to pass blame on a professor or the system. He could have blamed God as he mentions he was praying not to go on suspension. But he did not. That is a testimony of his parents' faith and the depth of his personal Christian faith and internal strength of his moral character. He could have given up and simply went for a menial job or worse with bitterness gone into a spiraling down life of trouble. Of course from the book title we know he did not do that. With faith that God had more for him in life he moved forward. He started at a local community college to retake the courses he failed. This time he had much better success with his grades. He also captured a new passion of Business Management so had a shift in his career direction.

Educationally he finished a Bachelor degree and then moved into success in the Business world. He then finished a MBA degree in Organizational Management. Finally he finished a PhD in Business. By this time his career path had shifted to desiring to be a tenured professor in a Business school. He shares how this came to be as well in the book. When he reaches that point in his life he also begins to have this dream of acting on the quote listed at the beginning by Dr. Martin Luther King Jr. That dreams is where he presently is focused on helping build up young people who care about the people suffering around the world.

Who would have thought a College flunk—out could have a continual spiraling upwards to being a professor in the story such as this? Dr. Moorer is a testimony that when faced with failure one does not need to stay in that state of mind and station in life. For him he kept dreaming and moving forward with an internal purpose in mind. The story shows the persistent hard work he put in to keep moving forward. At the same time another key to his success is his steady faith in his God that was a foundation to keep him moving in a positive direction. This is a story if you are an educator, you need to purchase his book and share his story with as many young people as possible. They need to be aware that failure will come but they need to be also aware they can move from failure to success. It is also a powerful story to help anyone dealing with failure to encourage them to keep moving forward with renewed dedication, passion and new dreams.

Wrapping up this chapter, I want to end with a song that epitomizes living a passionate life with purpose. It is a song that comes to mind about having passion in life and really digging into life: "Dig In" by Lenny Kravitz. When you have a passion-filled mindset that life is more like a party to enjoy rather than a funeral to suffer through you are Living More Than OK. I often use this song with University students to show them how to enjoy digging into their school life on campus. Yet if you go to the internet and search for the song and give it a listen you will see it really relates to passion in any stage of life.

The song makes you think about what gets you excited about living? Part of Living Life More Than OK is having something that energizes you. It is an engine that drives your purpose for living. For some people it is their career. They have a sense of calling about the job they go off to every day. For others they consider their job from a practical standpoint to pay the bills and their passion may be a hobby or a volunteer service they do outside of their job. Our passion in life helps us to dig in to life and make the most of this life journey.

There so much in the song to help us grow in life by reflecting on its meaning. Lenny Kravitz is a master musician, amazing singer, and a great lyricist. If we learn to be passionate about life even though it requires the hard work of digging we will have a good time. Also as with positive psychology, it doesn't say life is a warm fuzzy breeze all the time. Life has its difficulties but we are responsible to join in and create solutions that work for us. Sometimes life is unfair yet we can find solutions to redirect our reactions to life's unfair times. I especially like the reminder in the song that God is there to help us persevere when the mountain may seem too high.

Take a look at your life and see if you are digging in or allowing life to cover you up or give up on life. Come on in and join the party. Once you do you will have a deeper sense of meaning and purpose in your life with a digging in to life mindset. Living with meaning and purpose is how we are meant to live.

Reflection:

What are you passionate about in your life? What does "Digging into life mean to you? Write down a couple new passions you would like to explore for your life journey

Take some time to think over what are purposes that are driving your life direction? What is your career purpose? Is it a noble purpose? Outside of your work do you have a purpose or do you just exist? Consider a purpose you would like to follow to have a more than ok life and write it down with plans to follow a purpose driven life.

Take some time to write up a list of lies that you have are presently are telling yourself. How are these lies negatively effecting you life? Destroy the list of lies. Then also write down a list of truths about yourself. Post this truth list somewhere you can regularly see it. Also take some time to reflect on your bigger purpose in life.

What are some of your favorite flow activities? Are you learning more about that activity to keep increasing your

challenge level? What one new activity would you like to add in your life schedule?

Think over a failure in your past or maybe you are enduring a time of failure presently. What did you learn from the failure experience? How did it change your future? Also take note that Dr. Moorer's story keeps growing with new dreams and advancements. Is there a new dream that you have that you would like to pursue?

What ship are you presently spending most of your time on? Take 20–30 minutes to journal or draw your dreams of what battleship living looks like to you? What specific opportunity do you see in your ships telescope that is an area you can have significance in? Is it a particular cause or person you can spend more time with?

Resources for further learning:

Csikszentmihalyi, Mihalyi, Flow: The Psychology of Optimal Experience, Harper Perennial, 2008.

Damon, William, Noble Purpose: The Joy of Living a Meaningful Life, Templeton Foundation Press, 2003.

Covey, Stephen, The 7 Habits of Highly Effective People, Free Press, 2004.

Edwards, Dwight Tale Of Three Ships, Bright Sky Press, 2009.

Kravits, Lenny, "Dig In", *Lenny*—CD.

Aim For Natural Highs

In this chapter I want to look at not a principle of positive Psychology but ideas on how to have a better live. Practical things we can do to live more than just existing. An important idea to me is living a natural high lifestyle.

I came across this idea from my involvement as a Counselor in local drug/alcohol groups as a volunteer; for a couple of years meeting addicts one on one. Then also as I think back to my high school days knowing students who used drugs, their quest seemed in both cases to aim at getting high. They were bored and they wanted to move beyond more than ok and the booze and drugs gave them that immediate high, euphoric feeling that took them away from the dullness of their existence.

Back in high school as a Christian, I could never figure out drug users and those who drank alcohol. Even my oldest brother who was an alcoholic, as I observed him drunk, I did not see what the enticement was. Once in senior high school chemistry, I remember two students at my lab table were laughing about how they got smashed at a party saying how fun it was. One said he drank 12 beers. Out of curiosity I thought how one person could drink that much, so I asked how could he drink 12 cans of beer? His buddy laughed saying he threw up 3 or 4 times. They were laughing but I did not say anything. I just thought in my mind "what fun?!". I never enjoyed having the stomach flu and throwing up! It sounded like the party experience was like that! Who in their right mind enjoys throwing up??

In reading books and research articles on boredom I do know that one reason why people do alcohol and drugs, is they want that high feeling. They want the feeling of something beyond boring existence. They want the easy way to feeling excited and feeling better. The problem is the crash after the high involve headaches, grogginess, forgetting what they were doing while high, (which is often very foolish things). There is also the creation of an addiction to the alcohol or drugs creating anxiety, depression, paranoia, and criminal acts to feed the addiction. Consider also all the lives killed or destroyed by drunk and drugged driving. I remember always thinking to myself in high school as I considered the foolishness of drugs, that I would rather enjoy myself being in control of my full faculties and knowing what I enjoyed so I can do it again. Instead the chemical high places people in a mental stupor to do foolish and even deadly things to themselves and others all for the sake of fun?? I will take a natural high any day.

What is a natural high? From the website www.naturalhigh. org_they say a natural high is *"an activity, art form, or sport that you LOVE to do and makes you feel good inside; A Natural High does not involve drugs and alcohol"*. At their website they are trying to show alternative positive and healthy ways to go for a natural high instead of a drug induced high. Their emphasis is towards young people to show them non boring ways to enjoy life without drugs. I like that they bring up the subject of boredom; as in boredom research, life boredom, is one reason young people try drugs to give their body a sensation that they think is exciting. The natural high website provides testimonies that young people can relate to in encouraging them to go for passions in their life with activities instead of sitting around stoned on drugs.

Natural High was founded by Jon Sundt, who experienced the death of two of his brothers due to drug use. This life experience impacted him to make a difference to try to stop the destructive force of drugs in the lives of people. Personally, I relate to his experience, as I never tried drugs although they were readily available in the 1970's in my high school. That is because I saw my oldest brother struggled first with alcohol addiction and then drug addiction which finally disabled him until cancer set it, so thankfully it never appealed to me.

Mr. Sundt's Natural High Organization primarily targets school age children through high school. This is important to help stop the cycle of drug use and abuse. They provide testimonials of sport and music celebrities, who can be considered real role models. They share how through their personal "natural highs" they enjoy life. They also point out how their success is due to not using drugs. These testimonials show drugs are not needed to enjoy life like the lies of rappers and Hollywood media stars who try to delude teens that drugs are exciting and the best way to really experience life.

So what are some ways you can go for a natural high in your life. One important thing to realize is we do not need to be high all the time. As Lars Svendsen, a philosopher from Norway, says in the *Philosophy of Boredom*—boredom is. We all experience it. Life is not a Hollywood action movie. So much of our life is in the ok zone and can feel boring. Yet to have a full life and make the most of having joy in our journey and living more than ok overall, we need those high times. We need to realize though that natural highs are the way to go. If everyone is enjoying a life of natural highs there will be no need for the illegal drugs. Going for Natural highs will help lower crime rates and stop the senseless killings as we see presently in the drug wars in Mexico and around the world. For the addict they need to see what times and what feelings trigger the use of their substances in the desire to get high and replace them with activities, hobbies, and other alternatives to drugs and then go for the natural highs. For the non-addict as well, all people need to look at how to enjoy more of life. Explore hobbies and activities where they can find flow that can bring natural highs into their life experiences for a deeper enjoyment in life.

For new ideas on natural highs I encourage going to go to www. naturalhigh.org to learn ideas about natural highs. At that website you can view testimonials on the personal enjoyment of natural highs. One can also do personal brainstorming on natural highs that fit your likes and desires, there is no need for anyone to go for the false, damaging highs of drugs and alcohol. And I strongly say damaging for the individual addict, their friends, and family not to mention the cost to employers and society. That goes for marijuana too, the darling drug of Hollywood and the liberal media. I remember working with a student once who told me, "Sir they say marijuana is not addictive but they lie. It is" He had started smoking marijuana at age 12 and by the time he was in college he was hooked. He told me his addiction to marijuana had dulled his learning ability. It had also sapped him of his passion for a career. Instead the addiction tempted him to just hang around, do nothing, and be high. The best way to combat the drug problem is to give young people and everyone alternatives to drug induced highs and that is by supporting and promoting natural highs.

When I think of the travesty of drug use in people's lives I think of the musicians who have been destroyed by drugs. I still remember the death of singer, Whitney Houston, another extremely talented musician whose life was cut short. Her death caught my notice as I always enjoyed her singing as she had such a beautiful voice. When she died the main discussion in the news concerning her death revolved around her history of drug and alcohol abuse.

Some of the discussion in the news about Ms. Houston, was down right foolish to me as some wanted to use the sad event to promote legalizing drugs. How that would have helped Ms. Houston I do not know? Others were more thoughtful, I remember reading a Jamie Lee Curtis response on a Huffington Post blog presenting a passionate plea for a call to action, "I hope to hear the drumbeat get louder and louder, a call to arms to face addiction and alcoholism head on, to make the administration take on this epidemic and to utilize the media spotlight on this one addict's death to create real change." I felt she was right as Whitney Houston followed in a long line of talented musicians dying because of drugs; Janis Joplin, Jimmie Hendrix, Elvis, Jim Morrison and Michael Jackson. Of course add to this the thousands of not so famous people who die each year due to drugs and alcohol. Those deaths may not make the headline news but they affect the lives of their family and friends.

The Drug Testing Network lists on their website research that show teens are bombarded in TV shows, movies, and in the lives of their favorite celebrities that drugs are harmless and fun. I noticed an example of this recently while watching a movie where one of the lead characters was using drugs and the other lead character was presented as being jealous of that "Fun" lifestyle. If you have ever worked with drug addicts you realize it is not a fun lifestyle. Then there is always the common phrase "Drugs, Sex, and Rock n Roll" coined in the early rock music scene, which reminds us that drugs have long been a big part of that music genre. Sad to say many of these promoters of drug use have been in and out of drug rehab or have died from drug usage.

For years while I lived on the Border of Texas and Mexico I heard often the news on the drug cartel wars in Mexico. I believe the number of dead in Mexico is now up to over 26,000. I have stated before and still believe so, that the drug users in America and those who want drugs legalized have blood on their hands. Drugs are not essential for life and happiness. They provide a short lived false happiness with long-term destruction for the body and mind. Drugs are not the way to have a More Than OK life which I try to promote. Yet the drug users are fueling the violence in Mexico over drugs.

I have seen too many real life stories of the destruction in personal lives and families due to drug use. Most people can probably recall a friend or family member whose life has been destroyed by drug and alcohol use. I saw the destruction in lives in my volunteer work with a drug addiction organization in South Texas. I heard the stories of addicts whose lives were destroyed by drugs. From them I learned the reality that Marijuana is destructive. It stunts mental capabilities and destroys self motivation to improve to have a more than ok life. With the lure of the high feeling, people are seeking in going for drugs, the "just say no to drugs" does not seem to be the best way to stop drugs. For strong critical thinkers who weigh out the pros and cons of things in their life just say no comes across as the clear smart way to go. But positive alternatives need to be brought up for people to do to take the place of the "don't do" in the "just say no" slogan.

Teachers and Counselors in schools need to promote the naturalhigh.org website to their students and parents. Of course natural highs are not only for young people. Everyone should be searching out for ways to build natural highs into their lives. Living more than OK living is about having those natural highs in our lives to truly enjoy life as God would have us live abundantly. Being a bookhead, reading is definitely a high time for me as it expands the mind and fiction taps into the creative side of the mind. Music of all types also is a high inducer for me.

The key is to find the natural highs that work to make life more meaningful for you. Eplore new hobbies, prayer, meditation, build new friendships, seek ways to volunteer your time to a cause. These are the things that create flow in your life. These flow times create a sense of timelessness and enjoyment that are better than the drug induced highs. Build up the natural high times in your life and spread the news of going for natural highs. Instead of just saying no to drugs we need to point people to saying yes to natural highs.

Music is one of my favorite natural highs. Many will agree that Music has a powerful influence on people. At a music concert whether a classical symphony or a rock concert, there is emotion and power that you can feel in the performance. The power of music can also be seen in the positive effectiveness of Music Therapy which has been used with many different people groups effectively.

Music has been an integral part of my life. When my mom moved my brothers and I, when I was in first grade, into her mother's house there was a old upright piano in the back living room. My Grandmother would regularly play old gospel hymns and old time songs from the 30's and 40's. I always considered myself too awkward to play the piano as I have very little hand eye coordination, so I never attempted it. Musically I played trumpet in band through high school. Then in High School I started to play the acoustic guitar, singing and playing in church. Through my personal experience I have seen the effect music can have for the good in inspiring fans during high school football games and emotionally moving hearts and minds in spiritual worship settings.

I believe music can be for the good or bad an influence in our mental programming. I will focus on the positive and there are positive songs of abundance in all genres of music. That is one reason in this book I have been bringing up songs for you to further explore by listening to their videos on video sites on the internet. In that manner you can listen to the words and the music to understand the insight you receive from the song other than what I write about the song in this book. Classical music and jazz can be a positive influence in relaxing the mind and reducing stress. On of my favorite instrumental musicians for smooth jazz as I have mentioned is Keiko Matsui. Her music is often playing in my office as it is very soothing and relaxing for when I am working on reports and getting stressed compiling data.

For your own level of natural highs I encourage you to look into music. Is there a genre of music that you enjoy? I know of some people who make a playlist of their favorite songs in categories to relax themselves and other sets of music to motivate themselves during exercise or while working on projects.

When I think of the use of drugs or alcohol for that easy high feeling I begin to think about the word habits. Drugs and alcohol are bad habits as the regular use of a substance ruins the life experience of the user. Any habitual activity that creates negativity in our lives is a bad habit. Smoking cigarettes is another bad habit. My oldest brother died of lung cancer due to a life habit of smoking. It has been good to see in American society fewer people smoking. Those who do should observe someone dying of lung cancer so they can rethink that habit. Of course the decrease in cigarette smoking and the cultural shift in making cigarettes smoking a negative bad habit, makes me think of the absurdity of legalizing marijuana. Sure let's have smoke free schools, restaurants and businesses from cigarettes. Then crazily legalize marijuana where people hold the toxic smoke deeper and longer. The deadly elements of marijuana then absorb into the brain and remain there. Marijuana also changes the state of mind of the user where cigarette smokers are at least in right mind. Have you ever tried to hold a rational discussion with someone high on marijuana? It doesn't work. Of course the supporters of that drug just laugh and say that is the fun of it. Tell that to the family of the victim who had a marijuana user eat the face of the victim as in Florida some time ago. News media who likes to protect the marijuana lobby first promoted it was from being high on bath salts. When the true story came out that it was marijuana in the man's system, the news hardly covered it. It goes back to my thinking that being in one's right mind is the best way to live.

Thinking about habits turn my mind to the writings of Dr. William Glasser. Dr. Glasser points out these bad habits come about through people's wrong choices in searching for happiness. Their choice of drugs for happiness does provide initial good feelings but in the long term in the stories I have experienced their choice of drug and alcohol habits leads to misery. Dr. Glasser in his book *Choice Theory: A New Psychology of Personal Freedom* states, "If we can not create a society in which more people are happy, we will never come close to reducing these destructive and self-destructive choices," (referring to drugs and alcohol).

Knowing the personal ruin caused by drugs and seeing in the news the thousands killed in the drug wars in Mexico upsets me sa I stated earlier, when I see how Hollywood and some rock, pop, and hip-hop musicians glamorize drugs to youth. The lack of critical thinking in those who want something that destroys people legalized is sickening. In my eyes those who glamorize drugs and want them legal have the blood of the thousands of Mexicans and the thousands of ruined lives here in the U.S. on their hands. If only the media would place this truth in the face of those promoting drugs so people would stop using drugs; then there would be no demand for drugs therefore no drug war. The drug cartels would effectively be out of business.

In the meantime what can be done to better create a society Dr. Glasser is speaking of in the previous quote? Positive psychology is about presenting life principles to help build up happiness in people without having to turn to drugs. I see in positive psychology the emphasis on building up positive natural highs instead of chemical highs. Also as I have mentioned from my Christian viewpoint, I believe living a life that focuses on the spiritual helps in promoting natural highs as well, As we create habits that are spiritual in nature instead of popping pills and snorting chemicals into the body we can live happier and more fulfilled lives.

It all goes back to the habits we have in our lives. I had a sociology professor in Chicago who started out each lecture reminding us that humans are creatures of habit. Practically all we do in life relates to our habits. We take the same roads to work. We park in the same parking spot and become upset if someone is parked in, "our spot". I enjoy mentioning to students in my university success course there is no seating chart like in high school but if they notice they usually sit in the same seat each class session—habit. I had a Professor in graduate school one night after three weeks into the semester tell everyone to get up and change seats. Everyone was initially frozen as no one wanted to give up "their seat"—habit. So if we are honest habits control much of our living.

To have a more than ok life, to maximize our living, to build natural highs into our living, we need to evaluate our habits and make choices to create good habits in our life. Jack Canfield_in his practical book on life success, *The Success Principles*, has this to say about habits. "Negative habits breed negative consequences. Positive habits create positive consequences." I have never met anyone who admits to wanting negativity in their lives. Yet look at all the personal problems and relationship problems in life. Through personal choices many are creating negative habits with ruinous results in their lives and lives of those around them. So a bad habit is an activity ritually being done that is causing negative effects in your life. To get rid of the bad habits we need to choose to replace them with something else. That is one reason habits are hard to break. People just stop the habit. Since there is nothing to fill the void the person rushes back to the bad habit often defeated and building negative self talk of. "Well I tried and failed so I guess I just can't stop". So before stopping have a positive habit ready to take its place.

If you look into new habit creating on the internet most statements point to the need to do something 21 days in a row to create a new habit. I remember in the Positive Psychology class I took looking at the lectures of Dr. Tal Ben-Shahar emphasized the need to make a commitment for 30 days to get the new ritual habit firm in your life. So if you feel your are negatively affected by spending several hours a night in a habit of watching TV you may want to create a couple new habits of exercise and painting to fill up the time. Think of things you would enjoy doing that will have positive consequences in your life.

Another book by Dr. William Glasser important on this topic of natural highs is in his book *Positive Addiction.* In this book he turns the thought of addiction upside down. He points out that the word addict is thought of in the negative context of a life destroyed by drugs or alcohol. A person is weakly dependent on the substance to cope or escape from life's difficulties in search of happiness. In helping someone give up alcohol or drugs the drug should be replaced with something to fill the void, otherwise relapse quickly occurs. That is why the "Just Say No" concept of fighting drugs does not work. Dr. Glasser promotes, that to fully strengthen people they need to build a positive addiction in their life. Find something that they enjoy doing to bring happiness into their lives. Some of the positive addictions he points out in the book are meditation, sports, music and other art forms.

He points out from his research that ". . . positive addiction increases your mental strength and is the opposite of a negative addiction which seems to sap the strength from every part of your life except the area of the addiction."(pg39). If you think about it he is so right. Drug addicts are consumed by their addiction. There is often a negative effect in their work, health, and relationships. You don't hear of someone with a positive addiction of gardening going on a 72 hour binge of tending to their rose garden and not being able to function in their work because they enjoy planting flowers. Positive addictions help to round out our lives so as to help us function better is other areas of our lives.

Dr. Glasser's thoughts on Positive Addiction, coincides well with the organization called Natural High that I have mentioned. If every American would go to www.naturalhigh.org and consider building a Positive Addiction into their personal life there would be no more drug war here in the U.S. The Drug Cartels in Mexico would be out of business. People would then understand they don't have to ingest chemicals by smoking, snorting, or shooting up with needles to find happiness and relaxation in life. The personal destruction could end if we all could see that through positive personal interests such as relationships, sports, arts, nature, spirituality we can satisfy the human experiential needs for happiness and relaxation with natural highs that come from positive addictions. Will that ever happen? I doubt it with a liberal media and liberal Hollywood that promotes drugs.

One idea to enjoy life better is vacations. I am reminded of a cruise ship vacation I took with my wife, daughter, and my third grade teacher. This is one vacation I never thought I would do. In the past I always thought of cruise ships as people stuffed into an overgrown tin can floating in the ocean with hungry sharks underneath waiting for a snack. The idea of being on one was as enjoyable as eating a plate of artichokes. And I hate artichokes! So how did I wind up on the Voyager of the Seas on a Royal Caribbean cruise??

This all started one Saturday in the Summer when I attended a creative journaling seminar at El Rocio, a local retreat center in Mission, Texas. The seminar was led by Dr. Marsha Nelson, a therapist who focuses on creative therapy techniques. She gave each of us at the training a pamphlet about a cruise group to the Caribbean she was planning. I dutifully took one and showed it to my wife when I went home. My wife excitedly said, "we need to go!". Then my daughter overheard and was all excited, "Yeah! We are going on a cruise!" I was thinking, "Oh, great! Floating in a tin can for a week! How do I get out of this!".

I told them I would check to see if I could get off work. My perfect out! The cruise was during the end of the university semester so I probably would not receive time off. Well—I asked and I did get the time off.

When we boarded the ship, my wife, daughter, my third grade teacher, Mrs. Clifford, and I were amazed by the ship. The size was enormous and the décor was like a top scale hotel. We looked at the daily planner schedule and there were so many things to do, special classes on different topics from scrapbooking, to cooking, to better health classes. Each evening they have talented entertainment and music of all varieties throughout the day. The food was all deliciously prepared and you could eat round the clock if you wanted or would be able to. State of the art exercise facilities was available to work off the pounds from all the food. It was awesome to be working out on an elliptical machine staring out at the sea water with the sun reflecting its rays at sunrise.

All the activities and entertainment made it an enjoyable time. Also the freedom where my daughter could go off do her thing, my wife and my third grade teacher could relax poolside, and I was free to work on my writing and reading. Of course being a Bookhead I need my reading time. Yet the most enjoyable part of the cruise was the wonderful people on board. We came up from the Rio Grande Valley with the nicest group of folks that Dr. Marsha Nelson put together for the trip. Beyond our small group with all the friendliness between fellow cruisers there was no feeling of being alone.

I was also impressed by the workers on the ship. I could tell they were dedicated to great customer service. They went out of their way to serve and each person from those at the information desk to the dining helpers always had a smile on their face. Then the other passengers on the ship were so friendly. You could strike up a conversation with about anyone. I began to wonder if they slip a happiness drug in to the water supply? How else could the emotional atmosphere be so congenial?

Thinking about it further, there were several more probable variables other than a happy drug. One thought that comes to mind was the superb respectful customer service along with their friendliness of the workers helped create a climate in which the friendly spirit spreads throughout the ship. Another is that the type of people who go on cruises are more open to meeting new people, so that aids in the people on the ship having a closer sense of fellowship.

Another reason for the relaxed atmosphere is there are so many things you can do and no pressure to do any particular activity. Family members can do different activities or do the same thing. You can eat when you want, sleep when you want. So no one feels pressured. I have had several people tell me before taking the cruise that a cruise is one vacation where you go home relaxed and not tired. Many vacations I have been on you feel like you need a vacation from the vacation. I had to admit that I was completely relaxed after that cruise ship vacation.

Vacations are an important part of living more than ok. We need time to break away from our work and the routines of life. Vacations are a way to learn new things about the world around us, other people and people groups. This experience of being on a cruise has opened my eyes to a new way to vacation. I would encourage anyone now to be open to having a cruise experience as one of their vacations. I know my family and I will be trying other cruises in the future.

Exploring New Places can aid in natural high experiences in our life journey.

This relates to the story of our cruise experience. Aside from the delicious food, enjoyable activities aboard ship and the freedom to relax with a good book poolside; there were travel excursions offered at each Port of Call. These gave an opportunity to explore new areas and try out new activities.

Exploring helps us in breaking out of boring everyday sameness. The process aids in our knowledge of the world around us, increases our multicultural awareness, and increases our appreciation for life and history. Some of the activities offered on our cruise were snorkeling, scuba diving, and walking up a waterfall in Jamaica which connects with those who enjoy higher risk taking activities. I am a low risk taker so I usually am not found on those activities.

One excursion we did was to the Tulum ruins in Mexico set on a Cliffside with access to a beach below. The tour guide who was very knowledgeable on Mayan history shared how the Tulum site was an area for the higher aristocrats of the Mayan society and for religious purposes. From artifacts found buried the guide mentioned Tulum was a major trading center in its days.

We were lucky that our guide was not trying to be a Las Vegas comedian but instead filled us in with historical information about the Mayan culture and the ruins at Tulum. One sad item to learn was that at its height the Mayan culture had libraries with thousands of books. These were destroyed by early visiting priests who believed their culture to be evil. We were told of the mass of Mayan literature only three books survive today and they are in European University libraries. This story shows the importance of respecting other cultures.

The guide told us that it is still a mystery why a culture as advanced as the Mayans disappeared so quickly with no reason why. The archaeological excavations continue today as they had recently unburied another dwelling site. So maybe the mystery will be solved at sometime in the future.

Educational tours such as this one, is one of my favorite exploring activities. Looking at the layout of the small city of Tulum, I used my imagination and wondered what life was like in the 1200's when Tulum was in its zenith period.

Of course you do not need to go on a cruise to explore. There are sites all over this country to explore and around the world. In your local area where you live there may be small museums and historical sites where you can visit and learn from. There are many types of exploring activities you can partake in. I am emphasizing an example of historical site exploring as that is something my family and I enjoy. Here are a list of websites you can visit to peruse historical sites in the U.S.A. and around the world.

U.S. sites to see of historical importance:

http://www.historyplace.com/tourism/usa.htm
http://en.wikipedia.org/wiki/
List_of_U.S._National_Historic_Landmarks_by_state

World Historical locations:

http://www.worldhistoricalsites.com/
http://www.historicalsitesoftheworld.com/
http://en.wikipedia.org/wiki/World_Heritage_Site

Our journey on this earth is so brief and when you explore websites as those listed above you can see there is so much to do in life. There is no time to be bored with an ok life. We have opportunities in life to flourish and live more than ok in exploring the vast opportunities around the world.

Can exercise be a natural high? For the past ten years I have been consistent in using a treadmill and Elliptical for exercise most every night. Before then exercise was not a priority. It definitely was not a natural high. What caused the change? It is amazing how having two stents placed in two formerly 99% blocked arteries changed my perspective on life. The Cardiologist told my wife at the time if I had not been taken to the emergency room I would have died in my sleep. I wasn't that overweight. The artery problem was more genetic in nature as my father had died of blocked arteries to the heart at age 58.

When you come that close to death, life takes on new meaning. Especially when after the stent surgery I learned news of two people near my age that died of heart attacks. I reflected over why I was still alive when I stubbornly almost refused going to the hospital and possibly would have died that day. From the context of my recent thinking on living more than ok, I also thought how even though I am predisposed to clogged arteries my style of life of just being ok catered to junk food and lack of exercise in my past. My thinking had been, I am not overweight, so why bother with exercise.

After the stent surgery, I was placed in heart rehab therapy so was forced to go on a heart diet and an exercise regimen. Since that initial heart rehab after the hospital, I have kept disciplined in diet and exercise partly due to my wife's direction but also because I enjoy living life. I know I need to follow the regimen if I want to keep living. Another factor since that day when I could not breathe, as I felt like a thousand pound weight was on my chest, is a sincere belief God is not finished with me yet. I figured there must be a purpose for me to still be alive. My wife and daughter are in that purpose zone. But I believe even this book I am writing is part of the purpose. If I can encourage a few people to live a better life—it is all worth it.

One thing I have learned about exercise is that it gives you more energy to face each and every day. Since my time in the hospital I have been more aware of sensing my body. If I am sick and cannot exercise for a few days I can feel a sluggishness overtaking me physically. Recently I read in an issue of Scientific American Mind that exercise is not just good for the body but for the mind as well. Vigorous aerobic exercise helps keep the brain in better shape. So if you are wanting to live a better life and enjoy improved mental health become involved with physical activities as part of your lifestyle—jogging, walking, swimming, tennis, basketball, or treadmills can help in promoting a strong circulatory system. You can exercise by yourself, with close friends, or if you are a more social person you may find support in joining a health club.

Other than using the machines my wife came across a Walk at Home DVD series that we have begun to use and enjoy. It is created by Leslie Sansone, a walking coach. At first I did not think walking in place at home could be any help as a workout. We have tried it as a family and find it provides a vigorous routine and gets all the muscles moving. I still enjoy working out on my machines so we alternate as my family does not have to exercise everyday like I do. I highly recommend her walking dvds. Leslie Sansone has quite a variety of DVDs so we alternate the workouts for variety. Make exercise as part of your lifestyle choice. It is better for you to choose now rather than having a hospital visit choose it for you. You will be doing your body and mind a favor and it is a great gift you can give those you love—a better you!

As I am close to wrapping up this chapter an important way to find new natural highs for yourself is to explore hobbies. Those who enjoy hobbies can find that the hobby is a positive addiction that can give them a natural high feeling about living. My main hobbies are reading and music via listening and guitar playing. As an interest I share my wife's enjoyment in traveling and hiking. These activities add enjoyment and fulfillment to life.

Part of why I feel people live just an existing life of okness or turn to drugs for easy high feelings is that they do not have hobbies that interest them. How can a person learn about activities to get involved with. If you are looking for a new hobby interest in your life do a search on the internet. Here are a couple links that are helpful to the search for new hobbies I quickly found:

http://en.wikipedia.org/wiki/List_of_hobbies Wikipedia has an amazing list of hobbies to explore.

http://www.about.com/hobbies This website has at the time I am writing information on about 491 hobbies.

So as you can figure there are hobbies for every type of individual. There is no need to have a just existing life of staring mindlessly and wasting time with reality TV shows or other lame shows on TV. There is no need for seeking an easy quick high with drugs or drink that carries negative consequences in your life. To live a natural high life in living more than OK find a positive addiction and become involved in living your life abundantly!

With a full close of this chapter I want to bring another song to your attention. The battle between doing what is right in building natural highs into your life or creating a new mess in our lives relates to our personal choices. These little battles daily relate to personal choices we make. When we are faced with boredom we are faced with a choice how to overcome it or wallow in boredom until it deepens into depression or anxiety. We can also choose to react with risky behaviors like drugs that can create messes. Or we can move to living more than OK by choosing not to create a mess living a positive addiction life alive. The band Switchfoot has a chorus of one of their songs that goes:

I made a mess of me I wanna get back the rest of me
I made a mess of me I wanna spend the rest of my life alive
The rest of my life alive! (from the song Mess of Me)

The lyrics make me think of an important question to consider from Psychologist, Dr Shad Helmstetter who says in one of his books on choices. "Who knows what you could accomplish in life if you made more of the right choices along the way?". Drugs make a mess of you but natural highs are the way of making our lives fully alive. The choice is up to each of us. Listen to the lies of liberal media and liberal Hollywood types who promote the legalization of drugs or choose to aim for natural highs and enjoy the best life possible.

Reflection

Are there any negative habits dragging your life down to just ok existing? Write down two new habits you would like to begin in your life to better improve you daily experience.

Make a list of your top 5 vacation spots. Then go online and search for cruises that may go to one of those locations. Take some time to explore cruise websites to see what is all open to you in a cruise experience.

Explore the Hobbies websites listed or do your own search on hobbies and explore the variety. Are there new hobbies you would like to explore?

List your positive addictions that help you have a natural high in life. Take time to journal why these are important to you and how did you get started with doing these things in your life.

Reflection:

Take some time to explore the websites below on natural highs. Tell others about them as well. Then take 15 minutes to brainstorm natural highs you wish to go for in your life.

Websites on natural highs.

Make a list of your top 5 vacation spots. Research them and look at all the attractions available to enjoy at your favorite vacation spots. Take some time to explore cruise websites to see what is all open to you in a cruise experience.

View a couple of the above websites on historical locations and write down 5 you would like to visit in your lifetime.

Take 15 minutes of quiet time to write about one of your favorite exploring times in your life journey.

Resources for further learning:

Canfield, Jack, The Success Principles, William Morrow Paperbacks, 2006.

Glasser, William, Positive Addiction, Harper Perennial, 1985.

http://www.drugtestingnetwork.com/teens-and-drugs.htm
Website for the Drug Testing Network that has some important information on drug use and abuse.

http://naturalhigh.org/#featured-videos.html This website has stories of those who choose a natural high lifestyle.

http://www.walkathome.com/ This is Leslie Sansone's website to learn about her Walk At Home programs.

Thankfulness As A Lifestyle

Through this book I have not followed any set of order of importance to the ideas I present. That is because I believe we each are unique and various ideas affect us each differently. I assume each person who reads this book, (of course I am assuming more than one person will read this book at least—I hope!), will see one area that stands out more to his or her needs. Yet this topic in this chapter comes from a principle from Positive Psychology which I feel is of the utmost importance if we are serious about desiring a more than OK life. If we want to live the abundant life; a life that is continually spiraling upwards with positivity, we need to practice thankfulness in our everyday living.

Dr. Robert Emmons of the University of California has spent years of research on the topic of gratitude and thankfulness. His research shows that it is a positive benefit to our life journey. He says of gratitude in his book, *Thanks: How Practicing Gratitude Can Make You Happier,* "is the acknowledging of goodness in one's life, . . . , is recognizing that the source(s) of their goodness lie at least partially outside the self . . . one can be grateful to other people, to God, to animals, but never to oneself." (p. 4). There are good things in each of our life that we can easily see and that we need to be grateful or thankful for.

When we are caught up in the malaise of okness, it is easy to focus on complaining how boring life is. We then spiral into more negativity and get caught up in a cycle of just existing and the habit of complaining. Some complaining can be useful if it realistically is discovering a problem to solve, or providing an impetus to improve. Yet all too often we keep on with the complaining, and habitually gripe—that mires our thought lives with negativity. A positive way of breaking this cycle is to look at life with a grateful heart of thankfulness.

"He is a wise man who does not grieve for the things which he has not, but rejoices for those which he has."—Epictetus

"Appreciation can make a day, even change a life. Your willingness to put it into words is all that is necessary."—Margaret Cousins

"I would maintain that thanks are the highest form of thought; and that gratitude is happiness doubled by wonder."—G.K. Chesterton

The above quotes relate to having a grateful heart. Being grateful in our daily attitude is to focus on being thankful concerning what we have and the good things in our past that have helped mold us to who we are at this present point in time. Being thankful for parents, teachers, friends, and influential heroes that have shaped our present brings inner joy. This helps to counter the blame game of victimhood. Gratefulness for our present situation is a contentment that guards against complaining about what we don't have.

The sense of appreciation that comes from a grateful heart changes our life for the better. It can break the cycle of negativity if we are in the habit of complaining. Building the habit of a grateful heart will also affect the lives of those around us. For example, when you smile or say "have a nice day", to a tired sales clerk you can see an immediate body language change as they return a smile and say thanks. Try it on your next shopping trip. Give a smile to the worker at the counter and you will notice a difference. Too many complain, "That store clerk was rude"; "the waitress was so unfriendly". Maybe they just need a smile to remind them of how they should be. So our appreciative nature may influence others to be more thankful and happy as well.

The Chesterton quote pointed out to me that gratefulness can lead us to a sense of happy wonder. A deep spiritual joy can grow in our inner being as we look at the small things around us, and see how a simple thing like a rose in the garden brightens our day. Noticing the little miracles in life will lead us to having an awe-filled day instead of an awful day. We have a dear friend, who manages a birding store, in the Chicago suburbs. She gave us a Hummingbird Feeder on one of our Summer trips to Chicago. While we lived in Brownsville, Texas we had it hanging on our back patio and there was always a sense of joyful awe of God's creation as we watched our hyperactive little friends flitting about enjoying the nectar from the feeder. We appreciated God's creation as we enjoyed our morning coffee while watching the birds. We could also be thankful for a friend who through giving us that bird feeder opened up a new joy in our lives.

I have had my times in the negative complaining mode, so I can appreciate the experiential difference of living in a more appreciative mindset. I think back to the Positive Psychology class I took online with Dr. Tal Ben-Shahar's powerful lectures. His most impacting lecture on my life touched on the issue of gratefulness. It is helpful to see the research on the topic. He shared some of the work from Dr. Emmons that I started this chapter off with. From looking at the research it is seen that having gratefulness in our daily living has physical health benefits for better health, positive mental health benefits, increased happiness levels, and higher levels of personal success. That is what Living More Than OK is all about.

Many religious traditions speak to the subject of thankfulness and gratefulness. As I have mentioned in past postings, my spiritual heritage and personal worldview comes from a Christian standpoint of having a personal relation with Christ. Here are a samplings of verses on the importance of being thankful from the Christian viewpoint that have helped shape my thinking on the importance of thankfulness in our daily living:

Ephesians 5:19 & 20, "Speak to one another with psalms, hymns and spiritual songs. Sing and make music in your heart to the Lord, always giving thanks to God the Father for everything, in the name of our Lord Jesus Christ."

Philippians 4:6 "Do not be anxious about anything, but in everything, by prayer and petition, with thanksgiving, present your requests to God."

The two verses above are a couple of my favorites on thankfulness. Ephesians 5 speaks to our interpersonal communication that it would be positive in nature. Speaking to each other with Psalms and hymns with an attitude of thankfulness. Philippians 4:6 speaks of overcoming anxiety by the act of spiritual prayer in an attitude of thankfulness. We may not be blissfully happy about everything that is happening to us but by keeping a thankful heart we are better able to cope with life difficulties.

Viewing creation with a thankful spirit is a way I often enjoy nature outings on a deeper level. For example since we live near San Antonio we enjoy visiting the San Antonio Botanical Garden. Being in an environment where creation in all it's beauty is pointing to the Creator behind it all is personally inspiring. Visiting natural settings inspire a thankful spirit. You can enjoy a picture or painting of creation but seeing it live is always more moving of an experience. In art museums I tend to spend more time savoring nature works of art but they don't come close to seeing what the Master Artist/Creator does in nature. There is always such a variety to see and experience, from the rose garden, the Piney Woods area with a pond, the Hill Country wild flower area, and the Japanese garden at the Botanical Gardens.

My wife had some questions answered by the grounds keepers. The workers were very polite and were knowledgeable about the plants they tended. The worker we spoke with truly enjoyed his work at the Garden. My favorite area was the Japanese garden. They had gorgeous Japanese red maples and the shrubbery was neatly trimmed. In the Japanese garden area we took a rest from our walking. It was a quiet spot to simply, silently rest and mindfully soak in the colors around us.

Back to the thankful spirit that being in such a place brings to mind. As I savored our time there I first of all was thankful to the

Creator God who has given us such beauty and variety in nature. What if there were no flowers and just one type of grass and only two types of trees everywhere on the earth? Can anyone say boring? As we went through the San Antonio Botanical Garden in trees alone there was a vast variety. Then add the variety in bushes, flowers and rock formations. I was thankful for the variety.

Then being with family for an experience such as this reminds me to be thankful for my wife and daughter as I watched them enjoying the nature around them as well. I was thankful for a visitor from out of state who we talked to in the Japanese garden. Earlier she had overheard my wife wondering the name of a plant. Since we were sitting in the same area she took the time to share that it was an agave plant. I was also thankful for the dedicated workers who tended to the garden to keep it in such delightful condition.

I could have just rushed through the garden just to say I had been there, but by mindfully taking our time we fully enjoyed the total experience. From the most delicate flowers in the green house; to the cactus garden; to watching the turtles sunning themselves on a log in the pond, there was so much to be thankful for. When you go to a park, garden, zoo, or aquarium go into the experience with a sense of a thankful spirit and you will discover a deep restful enjoyment.

My favorite Holiday relates to this topic of Thanksgiving; as my favorite holiday is Thanksgiving Day. For many it is the forgotten holiday as stores and restaurants usually go from Halloween decorations right into Christmas decorations. Most likely in our commercial driven country it is because they make more money off those holidays. For many the meaning of Thanksgiving is lost in all the food and football. I instead focus in on the meaning of being thankful on that day

I always try to find some time during the day to reflect over things I am thankful for: My God and Faith, Mm Wife and family, a job as I enjoy helping college students, friends, my abilities in counseling, writing, and music, having a love of learning to keep my mind growing, Thankful for being able to Live A More Than OK Life. Thankful for the flowers outside of my window, where I do my writing. I am thankful to live in an era of the internet where I can share my ideas. I am thankful for anyone who takes the time to read what I write.

If we think honestly each one of us, even with all the troubles that come our way have much to be thankful for. I believe it is important to keep Thanksgiving day as a Holiday as it is a reminder to be alive is to be thankful. We need to rise above the humdrum of live and the troubles an notice there are good things active in our lives. The day should remind us the being thankful isn't just for that day but for every day of our lives.

Here is a Psalm of Thanksgiving from the Bible to reflect over. It was used as a musical song of thanksgiving.

Psalm 92 (King James Version)

¹IT IS A GOOD THING TO GIVE THANKS UNTO THE LORD, AND TO SING PRAISES UNTO THY NAME, O MOST HIGH:

²To shew forth thy lovingkindness in the morning, and thy faithfulness every night,

³Upon an instrument of ten strings, and upon the psaltery; upon the harp with a solemn sound.

⁴For thou, LORD, hast made me glad through thy work: I will triumph in the works of thy hands.

⁵O LORD, how great are thy works! and thy thoughts are very deep.

⁶A brutish man knoweth not; neither doth a fool understand this.

⁷When the wicked spring as the grass, and when all the workers of iniquity do flourish; it is that they shall be destroyed for ever:

⁸But thou, LORD, art most high for evermore.

⁹For, lo, thine enemies, O LORD, for, lo, thine enemies shall perish; all the workers of iniquity shall be scattered.

¹⁰But my horn shalt thou exalt like the horn of an unicorn: I shall be anointed with fresh oil.

¹¹Mine eye also shall see my desire on mine enemies, and mine ears shall hear my desire of the wicked that rise up against me.

¹²The righteous shall flourish like the palm tree: he shall grow like a cedar in Lebanon.

¹³Those that be planted in the house of the LORD shall flourish in the courts of our God.

¹⁴They shall still bring forth fruit in old age; they shall be fat and flourishing;

¹⁵To shew that the LORD is upright: he is my rock, and there is no unrighteousness in him.

The Psalmist reveals in verse 4 that being thankful produces gladness and happiness in our spirit. That is a positive result of being thankful. So if you want more happiness in your life cultivate an attitude of thankfulness.

As a Christian my thankfulness list placed God and my faith first. For each of us depending on our belief system the thankful list varies. For me in my experience the Most High God of my Faith has continually provided love and faithfulness to me. I have seen Him work in the past so I know I can trust for God's further work in my future. In verses 12–14 the King James version uses the word "flourishing" three times. Those who are thankful in union with

God will have flourishing lives. That doesn't mean riches necessarily but rather a richness and positive growth in our inner being that provides richness in enjoying and experience what I call the Living More Than OK life.

Each day take a few minutes to be thankful and see how it improves your daily journey in living a More Than OK Life!

Thankfulness enriches our lives by aiding in our positive mental health. Research reveals that people who are thankful have a happier outlook on life. They are more positive in their being. To have a thankful spirit we need to have an attitude of gratitude in our mindset as we look and savor life. One way to help in this mindset is taking time to be thankful on special holidays other than just Thanksgiving Day. As I write this I am thinking over Mother's Day tomorrow.

I think back to my mother who passed away many years ago now. Remembering memories of her on Mother's Day does not make me sad but instead thankful for whom she was. She was a devout Christian with a strong faith that she passed on to me. It was a faith that gave her hope while living through the Great Depression, working in a Rubber factory during WWII, having a husband who died much too early leaving her a widow with three boys. Still she never complained as she had a faith that God would take care of things. She was faithful to her church. At her going home celebration after she died one minister mentioned she was one of his most faithful parishioners. She wanted the best for her sons so encouraged education. My being a bookhead today is because she emphasized membership at the local library. She was always supportive of our educational journeys. As I savor memories of her life there is much to be thankful for.

On Mother's Day I think of my wife's faithful love and care for our daughter. Since our adopted daughter came into our life, My wife has had a heart filled concern that our daughter would have a bright future. Much of her growth into a young lady with her healthcare career in mind has been the fruit of my wife's motherly wisdom and encouraging her to take time to shadow workers at the hospital where my wife works. My wife's strong faith in God also is a reminder to me the importance of God in my life journey.

Below I have a poem by Helen Steiner Rice that makes us consider the depth of a Mother's love. It is a love that is sacrificial, and unselfish. It is a love that unconditionally is devoted to the objects of her love her children. Rice makes a point at the end that a Mother's love is a manifestation of God's hand in the lives of her children. It is a love that reminds all of us to be thankful for the mothers in our lives and to be thankful for the positive impact of Mothers in the lives of their families.

A Mother's Love by Helen Steiner Rice

A Mother's love is something
that no one can explain,
It is made of deep devotion
and of sacrifice and pain,
It is endless and unselfish
and enduring come what may
For nothing can destroy it
or take that love away . . .
It is patient and forgiving
when all others are forsaking,
And it never fails or falters
even though the heart is breaking . . .
It believes beyond believing
when the world around condemns,
And it glows with all the beauty
of the rarest, brightest gems . . .
It is far beyond defining,
it defies all explanation,
And it still remains a secret
like the mysteries of creation . . .
A many splendoured miracle
man cannot understand
And another wondrous evidence
of God's tender guiding hand

One way to grow in an attitude of gratitude and being thankful is to read stories and thoughts from others who are grateful. For doing this I highly recommend a book called, *On Gratitude* by Todd Jensen. It is a series of interviews about gratitude with artists, singers, writers, sport stars. I read five of the stories; Sheryl Crow, Alicia Keys, Daryl Hall, Ray Bradbury and Yao Ming. Each story from each person was different and they were thankful for differing reasons but I could see how being grateful had an impact on their life journey. The lesson I learned is we can improve in our attitude of gratitude by sharing and listening to others what they are thankful for in their lives. That is a key element to Todd Jensen's book. The author has a website where you can learn more about being a grateful person and the importance of it at www. thegratitudelist.org I would encourage you to check his book as well as his website out.

As I mentioned I feel Thanksgiving is squeezed out by commercialization. Thanksgiving is too often forgotten as a holiday and in our practice of daily living. I would like to continue the thoughts by reflecting on a song about thankfulness. It is a song called *Thank You For Today* on Phil Keaggy's Dream Again CD. Don't forget to check out his song on the internet.

The song to me is a positive reminder to live each day and even in each moment with a thankful heart. In the Positive Psychology class I took online with lecturer Dr. Tal Ben Shahar, the most important lecture for me was on the importance of gratitude. Phil is reminding us in this song that the main focus of our time orientation should be living in the present with a spirit of thankfulness.

It is not that the past or future is not important. The past is helpful so we can learn from previous failures in our lives. The past also relates to thankfulness, as I look back, I can be thankful for a mother who encouraged me to read and focus on my education. I am thankful for teachers, friends and ministers who were influential in my life journey. But if we allow hurts and hardships of the past to gain a hold on our hearts the past can crush our spirits into complaining and regret.

As for the future, I am very goal oriented, and I do believe future dreaming has a place. But is that where most of our focus should be? Focusing on the future too much can bring us to a state of continual worry of "what is going to happen?" A constant focus on the future can foolishly cost us by neglecting those who should be most important in the present—our family and friends. It can also cost us by our not doing our best in each present moment which can hinder our future potential. So Phil's song is right on the money in that right now, is where I am really living. I am learning to be mindful of keeping my focus on living each day to my best ability. The song is a reminder that each day can be a day of thanksgiving.

Reflections:

What is your daily time orientation? Do you live in the past? Do you live for the future? Or are you living thankfully mindful of each present moment? Take a short time to write down three things in your past you are thankful for and three things you are thankful for today!

Look over the past week and write down a list of as many things as you can remember that you are grateful for.

If you are religious what does God is Love mean to you? Think through the many good things in your life that God has brought your way often through happenstance events. How are you showing God's love to the people in your sphere of influence?

What does Thanksgiving Day mean to you? Write down a list of things you are thankful for in your life.

Reflection: *Take a morning or afternoon to visit a local park or botanical garden. Go into the time with a spirit of finding things to be thankful for. Later, journal how you felt during the time and how you felt afterwards. Did it increase your happiness level?*

Reflection: What does Helen Steiner Rice's poem say to you? Think about your mother and write down 5 things you are thankful for concerning her.

Resources for future learning:

Emmons, Robert, Thanks: How Practicing Gratitude Can Make You Happier, Houghton Mifflin, 2007.

Jensen, Todd, On Gratitude, Adams Media, 2010.

Keaggy, Phil, "Thank You For Today" Dream Again—CD.

Take a Risk For More Possibilities

I was listening to a message by a minister one Sunday day and he was exhorting people that God made us to be more proactive than reactive in our living. His exhortation was that we need to step out into the battle of life with more courage. His thoughts made me think of the need for taking risks at times in our lives.

Now me and risk taking do not get along too well. On Holland personality assessments I usually come up as a low Enterpriser as I like to play it safe and stay away from stepping out into the risk taking zone. Some time ago I read the book, *Take The Risk* by Dr. Ben Carson. In the beginning part of the book he reminds us that every day is filled with risks. That made me feel better. Maybe I am better at risk taking than I thought! Think of just driving in a car. When I see all the crazy antics that occur on the San Antonio highways I am amazed there are not more accidents than what there really are. Just getting behind a wheel of a car is a risk. Another example of risks I am reminded of is when we were at a hotel one weekend that offered free breakfasts. As I made the waffle I noticed a sign warning that the waffle grid was hot. Duh! How else does the waffle become hot and crispy! The waffle sign is letting one know of the risk of getting burnt taking out the waffle, (of course so the hotel does not get sued—remember the famous McDonald's coffee case!).

Back to the *Take the Risk* book. Dr. Carson shares stories from his life and the lives of his patients and shows how risks were taken so his patients could have a better life. I have read a couple of reviews on the book on the internet who felt the myriad of risk stories were overkill to fill up pages. I disagree. He is showing that risk taking occurs in numerous areas of our lives and we can follow the same plan in each situation to evaluate whether to take the risk.

Not every risk is the best thing to do. I remember hearing Dr. Krumboltz on the issue of risk taking and creating our own luck. He humorously mentioned if you take the risk of parachute jumping, you better be wearing a parachute. We need to think through the risks we take and not be foolish. Many senseless risks and ensuing injuries are caused by people not thinking through what they are doing. Which touches on the topic of critical thinking, I have discussed before. Think before taking the risk.

Dr. Carson presents a series of questions which I believe helps encapsulate good critical thinking before deciding on which way to go with a risk. I definitely suggest you read his book but here are his key questions you can ask yourself when faced with an important risk venture in your life. I recommend taking a piece of 8 ½ x 11 paper and divide it into four quadrants. At the top write what is the risk you are deciding upon? Then write these four questions in each quadrant:

What is the worst that could happen if you do the risk?
What is the best thing that can happen if you do the risk?
What is the worst thing that could happen if you don't do the risk?
What is the best thing that could happen if you don't do the risk?

Next go question by question and brainstorm ideas in the quadrant that relates a way to view the risk you are facing a decision on. As in brainstorming, just come up with ideas—they can even be zany. This is not the time to make judgments. Write down the possible consequences you may face.

After you have your brainstorming done; now put your critical thinking cap on and rate the ideas in each of the quadrants as to how important they are to your life. I even encourage students I work with to be even creative by writing a little story down of what you think your life would be like in each of the four quadrants. This may help visualize the better route to take. Do I take the risk or take the risk of not taking the risk, as even that is a risk. The key is you can have more peace about the risk situation if you have worked it through as to what is best for you.

Of course, if you are a person of religious faith then a necessary element is praying over this whole risk taking exercise as well. That will give you extra assurance that your God is guiding your thoughts as you reflect over the options. Through prayer often people gain a better inner sense of peace towards which way to go with a risk.

To risk or not to risk? That is the question. I believe those four questions from Dr. Carson can be a positive help in our being more proactive in living a more than ok life with the big risks that come our way.

When we do not step out in taking risks on new ideas or directions for our life we become stuck where we are. Stuck in dead end jobs, stuck in negative thinking of "I can't do this or that". The "stuckness" is often based on fear of what may happen. An illogical notion of only negatives can happen if we step out and try a new direction or way of thinking.

Of course using the risk questions of Dr. Ben Carson, it is right to take time to think of what may go wrong if you take a risk but other options should be looked at as well. The positive side of the risk needs to be considered. Too often new possibilities pass us by as we are stuck to the fear of taking the risk. We lose out of what great things could be ahead for us as we don't step out into the risk taking zone of trying for that new career, new learning experience, new relationship, or new hobby.

As I was pondering over this issue and considered the many times I possibly lost out because I did not take the risk to try something new, a song from the band, Switchfoot came to mind. The song is *Dare You To Move*.

Some of the thoughts that come to my mind are first of all I am glad on a personal growth risk issue not everyone is watching me as I make my decision. On the other hand, some of our decisions we face we need to realize people are watching. What can others learn based on how we respond to risks? I see the word tension in the song lyrics and when deciding on new options and directions there is a tension in our mind and spirit. Too often it is easier to stay comfortably stuck where we are or in our present thinking patterns. Then you don't have to deal with the tension of—What will others think of me? Instead of negativity couldn't it be possible when great things occur for you when you step out into a sensible risk, that people will think good of you?

What I like most of the song is the phrase, "Dare you to move". We need to dare ourselves to break away from the fear. If we have honestly worked through the Dr. Carson questions I posted past week and see the risk is a positive one; we need to dare ourselves to make the move.

Numerous times my wife and I have watched the movie, "You've Got Mail". As it is one of her favorite movies. I definitely recommend watching it. Each time we watch it new points of view come out. It is a great story, has a great emphasis on books and reading (from my Bookhead point of view), great acting, and many other great points to it. But in the movie at one point when the character Kathleen Kelly makes the decision to close her story; she is told, "you've made the brave decision. You're marching into the unknown!". How true of sensible risk taking. Even after you have considered your options and know deep down that the risk way is the best way fear is still there. So at that point we need to 'March Into The Unknown" and have faith in God who holds the unknowns in His hands. This example in the movie has much to speak to those today who are forced career shifters due to job loss and job cutbacks. But the march into the unknown relates well to any sensible risk taking venture and daring ourselves to move.

Many times in life we are too hard on ourselves. Thinking we should be the perfect student, perfect worker, perfect friend, and perfect mate. In the course I have mentioned several times on the Foundations of Positive Psychology the lecturer Professor Tal

Ben-Shahar_numerous times repeated the phrase, "give yourself permission to be human." What does that mean? I thought back to a student who had almost a nervous breakdown over a poor grade. It turned out the student had started out the first semester with all A's and then one class the next term started to slip which caused a spiral down in other classes. Why? Because the thinking that all A's was the way to be. There is nothing wrong with all A's but to hold oneself to that standard can cause inner turmoil and suffering. That is the tragedy of perfectionist thinking.

We ignore our humanness to our detriment when we pile up should and musts on ourselves in a unrealistic manner. I must have this job to be happy. I must have this person as my friend to be happy. I should get all A's to prove I am a good student. I often share how I believe we should dream big and aim for big goals to accomplish possibilities in our lives. Yet on the human side we should not beat ourselves up if we don't fully reach our dreams or goals. That only negatively tears us down.

Accepting our humanness can be capsulated in this quote by Reinhold Niebuhr: *"God, grant me the serenity to accept the things I cannot change, the courage to change the things I can change, and the wisdom to know the difference."* Being human is being content in areas that we cannot change. I cannot make someone like me. I can try to be more likeable. I cannot make someone hire me for a particular job. I can do my best in the job search and try to be creative in a competitive era of finding work. So on this journey in life understanding what we can change and what we cannot helps with the anxieties of the musts and regrets of should've and could've thinking that overtakes us. How much wasted potential is there when we dwell on the regrets of what we think could have been if we had that person as a friend or that job or whatever . . . ? As a Christian minded person I do agree with Niebuhr that in prayer we need to seek for wisdom to think critically over these issues in our lives for the right choices.

The acceptance of things in life, brings contentment and a life regret free; also the things we can change; we need to take the risk to change them. If meeting new people is important to you than trying out new venues of meeting new people such as volunteering for a social cause, taking continuing education classes, being involved in church or synagogue may be a new helpful change. If looking for a new career is an option then seek out a career counselor, polish up your resume, or start networking.

Accepting and understanding the need for change are things with we can do in our humanness. What makes these effective in our lives is taking responsibility. As I stated earlier I cannot change those who work with me. I cannot change my family members. I can only change me and that is my responsibility and choice. In Victor Frankl's book, Man's Search for Meaning, (this is another must read book), he says, *"In a word, each man is questioned by life; and he can only answer to life by answering for his own life; to life he can only respond by being responsible. Thus, logotherapy sees responsibleness the very essence of human existence."* So acceptance of our humanness is being responsible in our relation to God, ourselves and others.

A movie that we can learn much about risk taking is *Soul Surfer*. The movie is a true story and inspirational in nature. It is the true story of Professional surfer Bethany Hamilton, who hails from a surfing interested family. One day while practicing she lost her left arm at age 13 in a random Tiger shark attack. In real life she was attacked October 31, 2003 by the shark and then by January 10, 2004, she bounced back, competed in a surfing competition and finished fifth place.

Surfing is one of those high risk activities that I would never be caught doing because I am low risk. As well I have no sense of balance. Soul Surfer is a powerful story of resilience in the life of Bethany from losing her arm to not giving up and coming back to go on to be a professional surfer. The movie is based on a book that was written back when the tragedy occurred. The movie shows the range of emotions of her family and from Bethany. Being so passionate about the water and surfing it is understandable in a way to see her wanting to go back into surfing soon after having lost her arm. Then as she tries in a local tournament her failure catches the best of her and the disillusionment affects her life.

In the disillusionment period she goes with her youth pastor and youth group to help with the Indonesian Tsunami victims. Through this experience, in stepping back away from surfing it gave her perspective in seeing that without her arm she could still help. In this sequence there is a touching yet comical scene as she helps a little child overcome the fear of the water. Then coming back home she sees the mail from other handicapped people she had encouraged by her competing in the local tournament where she felt she was a failure.

There are various elements in her life that reawaken the passion for surfing. With family support and hard work on her part she trains for another competition. Her family helps out in her training and she doubles up her discipline and work in training to do her best. She does well enough in the next competition to keep her drive going to where becomes a Professional surfer.

Resilience as we looked at it in that chapter, is the bouncing back from hardship in our lives. In this story her spiritual faith is seen as one element in her resilience. She has her share of doubts from the standpoint of why would God allow this when she is so passionate about surfing. Also seen just how the positive side her spiritual faith and her Mission work in Indonesia gives her hope and expanded purpose that even though losing her arm she is possibly more useful in touching people's lives.

I would say her family is another element to resilience to help in her bouncing back. They were 100% behind her in whatever direction she wanted to take whether to stay in surfing or find something new. Of course they knew sea water was in her blood. It is touching to see her family cheering her practice on and then when she enters the competition. Yet she had to take the risk to go back into surfing.

The final element of risk and resilience I see in the movie is her discipline and hard work shines through. She is then able to take the risk to keep moving in her surfing. This is so important and is so lost in our culture. Hard work is not emphasized. People think success is about getting noticed on a reality TV show or promoting YouTube videos about yourself and lady luck is supposed to open the door for you according to the American idol culture we live in. In reality it takes hard work and passion. Before the attack Bethany's passion and hard work is seen and after the attack she knows that surfing is what she really wants hard work and passion is seen again. These are two vital aspects of resilience if we want to succeed in what we are doing. The passion is the motivator of the hard work and discipline.

This is definitely a must see movie from the standpoint of a positive story and what we can learn from it to improve our lives. I could imagine the change in peoples' lives regaining new drive for their passions if crowds were attending this movie and hearing her story of resilience and risk. Of course that did not happen. The liberal critics knowing it was a true story of a Christian did all they could do in their power to stop people from watching it. I read several online reviewers trash the movie simply because she is a Christian. Any critical thinker watching the movie can see the director does not go over board on the Christian angle. It had to be there in the story as that is who she is, but it is not overtly sappy spirituality. Other reviewers took a more mild approach, in their reviews, but again since she is a Christian harped with an opinion that it does not deal with real struggles and she seems to rebound too quickly in their viewpoint. Well it was her life not the reviewers. Plus I don't know what movie they were watching as you see the turmoil of emotions of the parents and you see Bethany's doubts as well. The truth is she did rebound quickly due to her youth, her family support, her faith, her passion and her discipline. All things we can all learn from. Reading the critics made me know why more people went to see a movie about a cartoon bunny that plays drums and a horror slasher film than Soul Surfer. Such a sad commentary on a society that definitely needs to hear the message and example of risk taking and resilience in this film. Instead people flock to brain dead cartoons and horror movies because that is what the liberal movie reviewers tell them to see. This is another fine, example of the lack of critical thinking in our American Culture.

Another way to explore possibilities in our lives and risks that we face each day is to explore our life story. Each of us on our journey has a story to tell. That story is our life. Many people enjoy reading biographies. These are life stories. I have noticed over this past year in bookstores many actors, politicians, and musicians have been having their memoirs written. With some honestly, I question what have they done to merit a memoir? Yet I am sure their fans will enjoy reading their story. The popularity of these books show the importance of story.

What about you and me? Each day starts out as a new page in your life story. As we reach major turning points and life shifts these become new chapters in our story. Family, friends, culture, government, life events, and our personal power of choice help to shape our story.

In Counseling Psychology there is a therapy technique called Narrative Therapy. It focuses on exploring story of a client's life. The problems we face are built into our stories and created by all the factors that shape our story. The solution to the problems is helping people re-author their lives in choosing to write new chapter directions in their story. A song by one of my family's favorite musicians, Matthew West, encapsulates the power of story and re-authoring in our lives. It is called *The Story Of Your Life by Matthew West*. I hope by the end of this book you are used to going to the internet and reflecting on the videos of the songs.

On our journey we face joys, pains, moments of weakness, moments of natural highs, and finest moments. In each of the moments we make choices that redefine the direction of the story. So we have the power to re-author our lives just as Narrative Therapy is saying.

Often in the painful moments we may become despondent and think our story is over. And sad to say some people make the choice to end their story. But if we realize our story is worth telling with all the pain and joys together, we can wake up each morning knowing a new page is turning.

I like the line that says "Cause it's a story worth telling". We may never have a book written about us or have a movie about our story. We may never make the national news either. Yet to those around us, our story is important. We have a legacy that will live on after we move on to the next world. What will that story be? Maybe you are going through a change, As I mentioned I recently moved so I have a new chapter facing me. What does that next chapter look like?

Fear is often facing us when we take risks. One day I was watching an interview with Jazz great Ramsey Lewis. In the interview he shared how he never considered himself as a composer. He thought of himself as a jazz performer of others' music. He stated that to him, Burt Bacharach and Duke Ellington, were composers not him. He then candidly shared that at one point he realized fear was a major factor in his mindset about this matter. He shared how this limited him and he felt more peaceful and more joyful about his music once he opened himself to accept that he could be a composer as well.

His newest album, Songs From The Heart, are all compositions written by Ramsey Lewis. In the interview I heard his feelings of fear about his being considered a composer. He shared as this new album came up he immediately started thinking of other peoples' songs he could put on it. It took someone else to remind him he had his own songs for people to enjoy.

Reflecting on the interview reminded me of how fear can limit our progress in our life journey and the dreams we are attempting. Fear can smother and weaken us so we give up on what we want in life. The fear may be of what others may think. Fear of failure in making fools out of ourselves. Fear of imagined negative consequences often chain us into being stagnant and not growing.

With anything new in our lives there will be fear. So with each new dream, each new learning experience; we will be faced with fear. The important thing is what to do with the fear. John Maxwell in his book The Success Journey quotes Dr. Susan Jeffries, "As long as I continue to push out into the world, as long as I continue to stretch my capabilities, as long as I continue to take risks in making my dreams come true, I am going to experience fear." Fear is a reality and we can't hide from it. It is part of the risk process in trying new things in life. We need to keep pushing out into the world on our journey each day. Fear keeps us hiding from our journey.

Another fear quote in the same book is one I have shared often with students, "The hero and the coward both feel exactly the same fear, only the hero converts it into fire." (Cus D'Amato). It is how we react to the fear that is important. It is about our attitude. Do we give up, or reevaluate and continue in a forward motion. There is nothing wrong about feeling fear. The wrongness is in letting fear control us and conquer us.

Going back to Ramsey Lewis, he conquered the fear by beyond open to his skills as a composer. He now has an album of his own compositions to share with the world. New songs that would not be here if he had caved into fear. What is being withheld from the world in bringing more beauty and joy into the world by our letting fear smother your dreams?

With vocal music the lyrics can be a positive influence. For example a song I often use at the beginning of a new semester with students is Tracy Chapman's *New Beginning*. New beginnings are scary and we have to be willing to take the risk to try new things in life. From a student standpoint, I try to encourage the students to choose some new beginnings for their habits as they begin life at the College. I share with the students how Tracy Chapman's lyrics fit well with the faulty beliefs some people cling to as noted by Albert Ellis' Rational Emotive Behavior Therapy. Ever hear people say, "My world's too broken, it's no use trying anything new." "No one understands the pain or struggle I am in." "Everything that happens to me is always wrong." Those are some faulty self-talk statements the song speaks to. The encouragement is that we can break the cycles of our faulty programming. We can start over again. I like how she says "We can make new symbols, . . . Make a new language, with these we'll define the world . . ." We need to encourage ourselves and others to make new symbols and new language statements for our success and living more than OK. As we change our mindsets to growth oriented we make new beginnings. As we change our negative self-talk to positive self-talk we make new beginnings.

In taking risks and looking forward to new possibilities we need to remember life is a journey and our power to choose helps to create the pathway. We can either trudge along stressfully with a woe is me attitude that makes it seem like the road is rocky and painful. Or we can glide along a happy trail attitude where we may still have rocks along the way but life is smoother as we make wise positive choices.

This thought of happiness through positive choices, is a focus of a book of short essays by Tal Ben-Shahar PhD who I have mentioned how his lectures have been a positive influence in my life journey. He is one of the leading thinkers of the Positive Psychology movement. I will always count it a privilege to have heard his lectures on Positive Psychology through a University of Pennsylvania Continuing Education online program a few years ago. His latest book I read while working on this book is *Choose The Life You Want: 101 Ways to Create Your Own Road to Happiness*. It is a grouping of 101 thought provoking essays for living a better happier life.

In the very beginning he reminds the reader that in each of our moments we have a choice to make. Each of our choices have consequences. He states, "what we choose to do and how we choose to think directly impact how we feel." When we are faced with difficulties we can choose to think that life is against us and continue in a negative life is a grey cloud pathway for understand rain falls on everyone and use the difficulty as a turning point to move in a positive direction. Some of the topics he touches on are: making a difference, forgiveness, focus on your strengths, look at difficulty as a challenge, appreciate good things, patience and success.

In the tiny book there are 101 ideas on helping you have a happier life.

His title reminded me of an old Roy Rogers and Dale Evans song, Happy Trails. Here are the lyrics:

Happy trails to you, until we meet again.
Happy trails to you, keep smilin' until then.
Who cares about the clouds when we're together?
Just sing a song and bring the sunny weather.
Happy trails to you, 'till we meet again.

Some trails are happy ones,
Others are blue.
It's the way you ride the trail that counts,
Here's a happy one for you.

Happy trails to you, until we meet again.
Happy trails to you, keep smilin' until then.
Who cares about the clouds when we're together?
Just sing a song and bring the sunny weather.

Happy trails to you, 'till we meet again.

The lines that stood out to me were: "Some trails are happy ones, Others are blue. It's the way you ride the trail that counts, Here's a happy one for you." This speaks to what Dr. Ben-Shahar is trying to get at in his book. Positive Psychology does not rule out the Blue days that some our way. But how are you riding the trail? Even on the blue days you can have a song in your heart or in other words work on positive choices that help the ride go more smoothly.

Does the person who dies with the most money in the bank and the most land have the most flourishing More Than OK life? A dear friend of mine in Arizona sent me a story about the Harmonica man. It was a video from Youtube and it showed a CBS news story of the life of Andy Mackie. He is a retired gentleman who lives a simple life in his camper trailer in Washington State.

He had numerous heart attacks and one day decided to stop his 15 medicines a day as he was tired of the side effects. He had a love of music, especially the Harmonica, so decided to use his medicine money to buy 300 harmonicas and gave them to children and gave them lessons on how to play. He must of thought that without his medicine he would die in a month. As he continued to live another month, he bought 300 more harmonicas and doing the same thing gave them to children with free music lessons.

Fast forward 11 years he had given out approximately 16,000 harmonicas. Since he lives simply, he even uses most of his Social Security funds to make a simple string instrument called a strum stick and has given them out to children as well. The report states with children in whom he saw deeper music talent he would even buy other instruments such as mandolins and guitars for them and teach them as well. Sort of like the movie and book Pay It Forward, other people became involved by sending donations to Andy. He was helped in forming a music foundation. His music foundation website http://www.andymackiemusic.org helps with giving instruments and lessons to needy children interested in music.

Here is the Youtube link to the news story about the Harmonica Man:

http://www.youtube.com/watch?v=PSpoMWQRCiU

Give a listen to the story as it is inspirational to see the fruit of his giving spirit. I like the principle he tells the young people that "music is a gift you give away". So he is passing his giving attitude away to the students. He also shares how the joy he receives from giving is probably why he has survived so many years after stopping his medicine. This mission of giving music away has been a foundational purpose and passion in his keeping on in his journey.

His story made me think of the scripture text in 1 Timothy 6:6-7, 17-19—"But godliness with contentment is great gain. For we brought nothing into the world, and we can take nothing out of it. . . . Command those who are rich in this present world not to be arrogant nor to put their hope in wealth, which is so uncertain, but to put their hope in God, who richly provides us with everything for our enjoyment. Command them to do good, to be rich in good deeds, and to be generous and willing to share. In this way they will lay up treasure for themselves as a firm foundation for the coming age, so that they may take hold of the life that is truly life." A life that is truly life is not all about building up possessions. The importance is on being content in life and using our money to be generous to others. We are not content if we are always in search to be the first on the block with the latest electronic gadget. Also this generosity is also not just writing a check but a generosity of good deeds. Such as Mr. Mackie's taking time to pass out the harmonicas and teaching young children how to play the instruments. It was a risk for him to follow the idea of giving away harmonicas but it has paid off richly in the lives of children.

Another item I want to make note of from my preceding thoughts is that the Bible text is not against wealthy people. In our country today there is too much disdain for those who have worked hard to gain wealth. These Bible verses do not castigate the rich. The Apostle Paul is firmly reminding them we come into this world with nothing and we leave with nothing. Once we die our toys and bank accounts do not come with us to the other side. So there should be a willingness to share a portion with those who are in need. Andy Mackie is obviously not rich but he is using wisely the funds he has to change lives of young people by opening their minds to musical talent and the discipline in learning music. We need to learn from his story to take the risk to give instead of comfortably hanging on to everything with a materialistic mentality.

If we want the best of this life we need to be open to take risks. Yet as we have discussed we need to make wise choices and not be foolish in our choices. Make use of the questions on risks that I mentioned from Dr. Ben Carson as they can be a helpful guide in any life choice you are making. In closing this chapter think over another song by Toby Mac. This song by musician Toby Mac which speaks to the importance of bouncing back and getting back up when life knocks us down. The non-risk taker folds and stays on the mat and lives a defeated life. The song for you to search on YouTube for the video is "Get Back Up" by Toby Mac.

In the song, words and phrases that relate to hardships and tragedies in my view were "middle of your nightmare" and "hit you out of nowhere". Often on news stories about earthquakes or tornadoes people will describe the aftermath as like a nightmare. Being hit out of nowhere is the experiential feeling we have as if the wind is knocked out of you as you hear of an affair of someone you trust. Also many going through hardships, bear scars that may always be with them or take a long time to heal.

The positive phrases that speak to bouncing back from hardships are "So get up, get up, you gonna' shine again" and "You may be knocked down, but not out forever". It is true during hard times we are knocked down. But do we need to stay down? No, we can get back up again. Although the darkness surrounding us in the hard times feel like an eternity as the song says we will shine again. Often we shine brighter afterwards as we build up our inner self and grow in resilience ability for future hardships.

There is a spiritual element I believe to going through hardships and that is what Toby Mac is speaking of in the phrase, "This is love callin". Sometimes in the hard times we feel alone and make ourselves more alone by pulling away from others. We become too caught up with "This is not fair" thinking. In that broken thinking from my spiritual perspective, we need to understand and be open to God calling to us with His love. Be open to the love of others He places around us.

I think through the hard times I have had in my life journey. I would never wish any of those times on anyone. But I can say each time I have bounced back and learned new aspects of my life journey in the process. Sometimes it took me longer to "Get back up again" and the hardest times, thankfully I had friends nearby to encourage me and often felt God's presence during the time. As I stated I am a low risk taker so considering this information has been hard for me. The times I have taken well thought over and prayed over risks the results have been worth the risk.

Reflection:

Think through a time of hardship you had. Write down what happened and what feelings you went through. How did you bounce back and who all was involved in the process? Fast forward past the event. Write down an event where you felt life was shining for you after the time of hardship. Be thankful for that shining time.

Think over a risk that you are facing possibly a job change, a move, a plan to go on for further education. Take a sheet of paper and work that risk situation through the Dr. Ben Carson four questions listed at the beginning of this chapter and see what you come up with? Write down what you felt about the activity.

Write down some of your thoughts about the Dare You To Move lyrics after you have seen the video on You Tube in relation to the topic of taking sensible risks. Do you have an area of your life where you feel stuck? Write down 3 Dares to yourself to Dare you to Move in new ideas and directions for yourself and your future.

Take 30 minutes in a quiet place to free write a new chapter in your life. Think through your present moment and where do you want to go next. What are some new possibilities for your story? Another idea—Go to your local library and pick out a biography of someone to read. It may be someone you know in history or just pick a biography by random and read their story.

Think through the music you listen to, what are your favorite songs? Are you choosing music that builds you up. Google the lyrics of your favorite songs and see what the lyricist is saying and how it applies to your life.

What is your level of contentment in life? Are you chasing after materialism? Do you have a passion you can teach to young people or those young at heart? If you attend a church can you volunteer to serve generously with the talents you have? Is there a community group you can contribute some of your monetary and volunteer time to?

Resources for Future Learning:

Ben-Shahar, Tal, Choose The Life You Want: 101 Ways to Create Your Own Road to Happiness, The Experiment, 2012.
Carson, Ben, Take The Risk, Zondervan, 2008.
Frankl, Victor, Man's Search for Meaning, Beacon Press, 2006.
Mac, Tobey, "Get Back Up", Tonight—CD, 2010.
Maxwell, John, The Success Journey, Thomas Nelson, 1997.

Final Thoughts

Thank you for joining me on the journey of Living More Than OK: Spiraling Up To Abundant Living. I hope it is not a letdown that I have not solved all of society's problems with this book. As you wake up tomorrow there will still be big government trying to overreach to control our lives. There will still be economic problems through the world. With the lack of concern for persons with deep mental health problems there will still be mass killings. You name it, the problems will continue as long as people settle for existing in what they think is OK. I would like to say society as a whole will change. I don't see it happening. Only if people would demand the government to be a servant instead of the all controlling power that passive voters have allowed it to become will American society change. Only if a majority of voters would seek to become creators rather than victims reaching out for handouts can society change. With recent elections I do not see that mentality changing as a whole. That does not mean you personally cannot rise above the problems.

My hope is that you will see you don't have to live for merely existing in life. You can keep growing spiritually, mentally and emotionally. Don't settle for the plateaus of OKness. Keep open to dreaming big and have openness to positive opportunities that some your way. There is so much God given potential in each person. We need to make the choice to tap into that potential to live beyond OK to Living More Than OK. Do stop by my blog www.livingmorethanok.blogspot.com from time to time to gain more ideas to keep spiraling up to positive growth in your life!

Edwards Brothers Malloy
Oxnard, CA USA
December 9, 2013